Your Cheater Keeps Cheating —And You're Still There!

By

DR. GILDA CARLE

America's Favorite Relationship Expert

ISBN: 978-1-881829-22-5

Library of Congress Control Number:
2018951722

Printed in the United States

For more information visit
www.DrGilda.com

♛

Gilda-Gram®
The first time a cheataholic cheats
is never the last.

ACKNOWLEDGMENTS

Thank you to all who have so generously contributed your true stories to help others who are reading this book. Without your giving, there would be less healthful living!
--Dr. Gilda

PREFACE

I have been studying the topic of love, relationships, and infidelity for years. I have written many books, authored many columns, appeared on many TV and radio shows, been quoted in many international newspapers and magazines, and I have a private online practice that ministers to people's wounds in real immediate time. As you will see, some of the research I've done for this book draws from news stories as far back as the early 2000s.

Sadly, the hurt and pain inflicted from infidelity is still very current. What has really changed between then and now? Only the names and bodies and specifics are different. The betrayals, the family dysfunctions, and the angry communication is raw and real to anyone going through lies in love.

This book explores why cheaters keep cheating—but more importantly, why you continue to hang around. The answers may be different for different people. Identify some of the common threads that are true for you, and please turn the corner onto the street of emotional wellness. It's your glorious life!! If you need help, just reach out!

Love, (of course)
Dr. Gilda

Table of Contents

PART I: INTRODUCTION

Anatomy Of A Cheataholic

cheataholic, *n.* 1. *Sl.* love junkie. 2. person addicted to hidden passions, secret flirtations, and illicit romances behind the back of an unsuspecting partner. 3. *Biochem.* person who repeatedly seeks the rush of exhilaration that accompanies falling in love.

Everyone wants love. Psychologist William James said, "The deepest principle in human nature is the craving to be appreciated." And Neapolitan author, Liciano de Crescenzo, said, "We are each of us angels with one wing, and we can only fly by embracing each other." So, when actor Sean Penn revealed that he didn't feel he'd ever been loved, despite his two marriages to beautiful and talented performers, Madonna and Robin Wright, the sadness was palpable.

Most people believe that once they find love, they've secured their ticket to paradise. They will

Khloe admitted how it emotionally tore at her dad when he found out.

Yet, history repeated itself when she partnered with ex-husband, Lamar Odom, who admitted to having "multiple affairs with different women" while the pair was married. When she moved on to Tristan Thompson, with whom she had a child, he was caught cheating with an Instagram model. Perhaps it was because she was so used to and even numbed by all the infidelities around her, she decided to stay with him and attempt to rebuild what they had.

Another of the Kardashian clan's sisters, Kim, was accused by her first husband of having multiple affairs. Kylie Jenner, another sister, was allegedly faced with beau Tyga's cheating scandal with a 14-year-old model.

And Scott Disick's cheating finally ended his relationship with Kourtney Kardashian with whom he has 3 kids.

Excuses like "sex addiction," "misunderstandings," and "I-should-have-kept-it-in-my-pants" were bandied about. But the humiliation and pain caused by each indignity will have lasting effects not only on the cheaters and the cheated, but on their children, as well.

YOUR CHEATER KEEPS CHEATING
—AND YOU'RE STILL THERE!

Cheating exists everywhere, even in the top tiers of government. The Governor of New York had to leave office in disgrace because he had been a repeat procurer of prostitution businesses over the course of at least six years, and possibly 10. When he made his resignation speech, his pained wife stood at his side, looking shell shocked and wooden. (They are now divorced.) The media buzzed about the scandalous irony of a hard-nosed official who prosecuted the very kind of businesses he patronized.

The issue of hookers in Governor Eliot Spitzer's bed was just the side attraction. The real issue was that his marriage was in trouble—and neither he nor his wife ever acknowledged this truth. When issues are not dealt with, they usually blow into dishonors far worse than the original problem.

Based on the now defunct anthropological concept that passion lasts for just a finite period of time (because it's now been found that passion can last indefinitely), I conceptualized relationships as having two separate parts. Each one requires a unique set of skills that must be dealt with differently:

Phase I: The Discovery Phase

This is the stage of Passion Acceleration. It involves out-of-control lust that entails the thrill of discovering the unknown. In the scope of a lifetime

together, this period will last a comparative short
amount of time. A twosome like the former couple,
Jude Law and Sienna Miller, would expand its shelf
life by continuing to inject drama, break-ups, make-
ups, and media coverage into the merger. By June
2006, Star Magazine had counted the couple's stops
and starts to be four since their engagement in
December 2004! Imagine what two years of such a
roller coaster romance can do to the nerves!

In November 2005, the tabloids pegged Sienna
behind Jude Law's cameo in her new movie,
"Factory Girl." Rumor had it that Sienna wanted to
keep Jude close to her to stave off his wandering
eye—as though any partner could legislate such a
thing. The couple continued to have rip-roaring
fights, which their friends said, helped to spice up
their sex lives. But that kind of relationship wears
people thin. Finally, in November 2006, Law pulled
the plug. Insiders said that Sienna partied too much,
and that Jude, being a "devoted father of four
children," decided that "all this going out" was not
for him. Today, they are with different partners.

Non-celebrity couples also argue, separate, and
merge, to spice up their passion, like this Hollywood
duo. This approach to longevity works in some
cases. For example, the ups and downs of unions like
Madonna and Guy Ritchie seemed to build fanfare
and publicity from their marital drama. And Pamela
Anderson and Kid Rock dated and broke up many

times before they married—and then divorced. They ended their engagement the first time in 2002.

But after Pamela was assured that Kid Rock had stopped being a player, they tied the knot—with four different wedding celebrations. When In Touch Magazine readers were asked whether they thought the Pamela/Kid Rock marriage would last, 62% said "No." One reader joked, "She's already married to her boobs—they're supportive and never talk back." How true that might have been!

While the couple had been screening the humorous movie, Borat, in which Anderson had a part, Kid Rock threw an angry tirade, furious about his wife's role in it. Obviously, there had been a reason the pair had continued to date and break up before finally marrying. But the union lasted for only a blink-and-you'll-miss-it moment. In the end, the number of wedding celebrations they had was the same as the number of months they were married— only four!

♛

Gilda-Gram®
Passion in a hot, flirtatious affair will not work the same way in a stable marriage.

While 72% of Us Weekly readers vowed they would not marry an ex, for celebrities, the media attention boosts the attractor factor—as long as the couple doesn't take the criticism too much to heart. Non-celebrity couples living without the limelight are left to handle their issues devoid of fanfare and the egging on of fans. If a marriage or cohabitation lasts for say, 20 years, only Years One to Three can possibly comprise the Part I Discovery Phase. While people are involved in this stage, they are under the spell of romantic bliss, and there is no skill required to obliviously walk into walls.

Phase II: The Discovered Phase

This is the stage of Passion Deprivation. It is the second stage of relationships, which accounts for the bulk of time two people actually spend together. It's beyond the breathlessness in bed. It's beyond the "I-Can't-Wait-to-See-You" excitement. Beyond the initial romantic suspense, this phase comprises the remaining years people spend together after Discovery. It is typically a period of Passion Deprivation because this phase no longer boasts the new and the unknown. So now some special skills are required to keep it going as the suspenseful, breathlessness is exchanged for comfortingly dependable, blah routine.

People often take the waning heat personally, and they unknowingly try to resurrect their feelings of self-worth in whichever way they can. The attempt often results in cheating, but cheating can never re-install someone's self-worth. So, a cheater will cheat again and again and again, thus becoming

7

addicted to his/her vice, forever seeking the thrill
s/he had during Phase I.

A couple involved in any relationship of any
duration needs to understand the cheataholic's
motives, turn-ons, and concerns. It's more about
self-stroking than it is about sex, and it's more about
self-preservation than it is about the person the
cheater cheats with or the one s/he cheats on.

♛

Gilda-Gram®
Your potential for ongoing passion
is directly proportional to your love for
yourself.

Note to Readers: All the stories and emails in this
book are real. But the names and circumstances
have been changed to protect the guilty and the
suffering.

YOUR CHEATER KEEPS CHEATING
—AND YOU'RE STILL THERE!

Throughout time, experts have agreed that the motives for cheating are many and varied. Some of them include:

- the cheaters' friends are doing it, and they want to be one of the crowd

- this is the behavior they saw adults enacting when they were growing up

- they're thrill-seekers, grasping for adventure, excitement, and danger

- they're angry at their partner—or their mother or father, dating back to their youth

- they are resentful because they live with spousal apathy

- they secretly want to get caught so they can begin to patch up their marital woes

- they feel bored, or suffocated, or abandoned by their partner, and they seek high excitement with low-involvement ego stroking

- they are self-involved, narcissistic, and hedonistic, and willing to sacrifice family commitments

- they feel that what they have in life is undeserved, so they're willing to sabotage it

- they are in power positions, and they feel entitled

- they feel inadequate, and they need to feel accepted

Or, they simply defer their adulthood, and put off growing up. This unusual personality assignment was named "rejuveniles," the title of a book by Christopher Noxon. It describes middle-aged people who feel too childlike to commit or settle down.

Sure, these factors do contribute to cheating behavior. But I have noted a common thread among cheaters that has not been explored: *a desperate urge to reclaim the hot and wild passion once enjoyed.*

It has been reported that one episode of the old kind of sex could last 20 to 30 minutes, burning 300 calories. But the usual, dull routine lasts only two to six minutes, and expends only 25 calories. Such is the price of dullness. Could this be one reason married people also tend to weigh more?

Whatever the reason, there is often this push to reclaim lost passions—and it usually involves a partner outside the relationship. The plentiful inducements that exist support even just the thought of transgressing. In their song, "Don't Cha,'" the Pussycat Dolls tease,

Don't 'cha wish your girlfriend was hot like me?
Don't 'cha wish your girlfriend was free like me?
Don't 'cha wish your girlfriend was wrong like me?
Don't 'cha wish your girlfriend was fun like me?

YOUR CHEATER KEEPS CHEATING
—AND YOU'RE STILL THERE!

Don't 'cha? Don't 'cha?

Six hot Dolls prance on stage in abbreviated outfits and abundant curves seducing, beckoning, inviting. Their popularity soared so high that toy manufacturer, Hasbro, planned to model a set of them after the pop band. But the plans were dashed after parents protested the group's scantily clad seductions. Despite what the parents' motives were, don't 'cha think a lonely dad who hasn't felt the embers of burning passion at home for some time might have enjoyed toying with one of these Dolls himself?

Passion is the engine of life. It is the thrill that drives us, and the force within that gets us excited about each new breath we take. It is the fresh, eager feeling of delicious expectancy. Without it, we aren't much motivated to go on. So, what happens after settling into the routines of life?

In too many marriages, once the honeymoon ends, so does the sex. Sex among mosquitoes lasts a paltry two seconds. Married people have complained to me about their own reduced lovemaking time, especially compared to what they used to have. Marrieds, in fact, spend almost 10 minutes less on each sex act than those who cohabitate.

Further, the average married couple has sex 68.5 times a year, or slightly more than once a week. So, the once-steamy sexual relationship a couple had four times a week may turn into a paltry once every two weeks—if they're lucky. It is estimated that 15 to 20% of couples have sexless marriages, defined by sexual activity 10 or less times a year.

Overall, less than 50% of Americans say they are sexually satisfied, with 20 to 30% of men saying they have little or no sex drive, and 30 to 50% of women declaring the same. Zsa Zsa Gabor said, "I know nothing about sex because I was always married."

Zsa Zsa's comment may ring truer today than ever before as our busy life schedules become more difficult to maintain. A hippo's scream during sex has been recorded at 115 decibels louder than a jet take-off. And during mating periods, lions copulate 20 to 40 times a day. When was the last time you heard any human brag about such intense passion?

By Melanie's own admission, her romance with her husband never enjoyed that kind of heat. In fact, she described her marriage as dead. Yet, at 59, her husband wasn't prepared to end his vital life. He believed he should cram whatever time he had left into a passionate new beginning with someone who would look for more than life in a retired easy chair. So, he left her for someone young and new, and Melanie was distraught, never quite understanding why.

♛

Gilda-Gram®
Sex is the calling card of passion.

Age never has to be a factor in how a person deals
with his/her sexuality. If a person feels passionate,
s/he feels sexy. Ninety-year-old producer David
Brown, winner of four Oscars, and husband to Helen
Gurley Brown for over 50 years, once said that sex
held so much "power," he warned, "One strand of
pubic hair can be stronger than the Atlantic cable."

Melanie questioned what she had done *wrong* in
her marriage. The answer was "nothing"—that is,
that she did wrong. Melanie was not a bad person.
But the truth was, she did absolutely "nothing" to
spark or re-spark the embers that had died in her
marriage years earlier. Like Melanie, most partners,
as well as the cheaters themselves, take their lost
passion personally, concluding not that love doesn't
last, but that it is *they* who can't hold onto it.

Feeling unloved is a primary wound for all
people. The emotion it ignites is fear, and the
behavior it manifests consists either of suppressing
emotions inside yourself or acting your emotions
out. Acting in consists of depression and self-
loathing. Acting out consists of an often-
unconscious search for an ego charge in a new
partner.

14

So, in either case, fear is used to forecast doom and gloom rather than to sound a needed alert that something is wrong and must be addressed at once. Instead of picking up the cues that change is needed, many people try to stave off their fear by running from it—by cheating.

Robert's four-year relationship lacked its original fervor. Typical of many people frustrated by this usual fact of life, he went out behind the back of the person he was living with, and found someone new whom he thought had all that was missing from his current relationship. New people usually do provide excitement, but not because they are so much better. It's simply because they are new.

But this guy wanted to hedge his bets, hoping that if the new love didn't work out, he'd be able to keep the one he already had. He was especially worried now because he was getting older. This guy desperately wanted promises that his fading youth would bring him love and companionship—*as though anyone's life can provide guarantees!*

Since new passion has a shelf life, too, this guy would undoubtedly need to be searching again for someone who could duplicate the passion he lost after his new love became an old love. This is how cheating becomes a chronic and addictive drive that doesn't end. This drive is what I call "cheataholism." It's based on the notion that, like the

Whether it was in Einstein's day, before that, or in today's current society, after most people become comfortable, they fall into their routine habits and take their relationship for granted, minimizing or ignoring the needs of their partner, the same needs they bent over backwards to meet while in the throes of courtship. Whether this is true or not, a shoe advertisement claimed that 37% of all women preferred shoe shopping to sex. That hurts more than bunions!

In reality, enacting the same habits day in and day out can lead to boredom, and eventually, the desire to look outside the relationship for what used to be enjoyed with the person you are with. As one cheataholic revealed, "I have been happily married for 45 years. It's just that I am a hunter, and from time to time I like to shoot," he defended. What was his wife's reaction to his admission? She said she is standing by her man, "as I have always done in difficult times." She's not the only mate of a cheataholic who has chosen this stance.

New York Daily News, July 28, 2006, The 81-year-old father of Minnesota Sen. Norm Coleman was caught having sex with a 38-year-old woman in a St. Paul pizzeria parking lot on Tuesday. Cops cited Norm Coleman Sr., a longtime Brooklyn resident, for engaging in "lewd and disorderly conduct" with Patrizia Schrag, who told police Coleman Sr. was her "boyfriend." Coleman's wife, Beverly, who lives

YOUR CHEATER KEEPS CHEATING
—AND YOU'RE STILL THERE!

*in New Jersey, told the St. Paul Pioneer Press
her husband "suffers from symptoms" of
Alzheimer's disease. Obviously, he remembers
how to do some things...*

Besides hanging in with your unfaithful partner, a new, more controversial approach is to affair-proof your relationship in advance by agreeing to confess temptation as soon as you feel it. At various retreats and workshops, couples have been building trust through explicit spoken or written agreements before action toward cheating occurs. So, if either person has the urge to stray, they discuss it with each other first. Couples say that telling their spouse about such a desire tends to quash it. Peculiarly, this may make sense, since much of the lure of infidelity is the secrecy and sneaking around.

Many people believe that once a spouse has strayed, that's the end of the relationship. But a union doesn't necessarily have to terminate because of infidelity. In fact, it has been found that 65% of couples remain together after one or both of the pair cheated.

But a couple must take stock of what was going on in the relationship that bored the daylights out of them that sparked an interest in finding someone new. They must honestly discuss it, and then decide on alternate ways to make each other happy.

Usually, people chalk up common boredom with their mate as a "lack of communication." But the issue lies a lot deeper than what it appears to be. The General Social Survey, one of America's longest-running assessments of social, cultural, and political issues, revealed that a whopping 25% of its respondents felt they had no one to talk to.

Those who said they relied on their spouses for conversation regarding important matters grew from 5% in 1985 to 9% in 2004. What? Only 9% of couples feel comfortable confiding in their mates? What about the 91% of marrieds who do not feel close enough to their partners to share confidences? How isolated these people must feel, living under the same roof with someone, yet unable to communicate openly about their deepest thoughts and feelings.

There is a gaping wound in a relationship where you cannot share your soul with your "*sole mate*." Surely, everyone needs a confidante. The New York Times called our culture's social isolation a "Confidante Crisis." I call it a "Crisis in Uncloseness." Especially in the case of people who are married, in who do these partnership isolates confide?

Outside a committed relationship, ordinary interactions consist of superficial, functional mergers that serve a purpose when the need arises. However, in relationships that are presumably more intimate, many people still remain unfulfilled in their desire to be known in a deeper way. Yes, most people crave skin-deep love, similar to a tiger's stripes.

♛

Gilda-Gram®
Tigers have striped skin,
not just striped fur.

In an effort to get to the skin part, rather than remain in the nappy surface hair, our culture has invested in a lot of Social Networking in an effort to join someone's select group. But the perceived safety behind the computer screen seems to be as far as many people are willing to venture. So where is the adventure? Where is the growth? Where is the reaching beyond the comfort zone?

An interview in The New York Post with Joseph Epstein, author of "Friendship: An Expose," revealed that men rely on their wives to be their best friend far more than women rely on their husbands. So, it is no wonder Nick Lachey, freshly out of his marriage to Jessica Simpson, said, "I'm a romantic at heart. I don't want to be a serial marrier, but at the same time, I can't imagine not being married again."

Epstein says, "Men don't find confidantes that easily. I think men feel that women are going to judge them less in some way." Women, of course, have girlfriends with whom they experience self-revelation, which men don't duplicate with other men.

Epstein calls the byproduct of friendship, "affection," while the byproduct of love is "passion." He says, "Sex can only f--- up a friendship. On the other hand, marriage is often about sex. But I think if you have a great, passionate relationship, it's wonderful, but it's not quite a friendship. Sex is passion, and friendship's affection. They only emerge and merge over time," which is my point, precisely.

The major question, then, is "How patient are people willing to be to get to that 'emerging' and 'merging' point?" Most often, in our instant and disposable society, couples have the attention span of a gnat, and are quick to throw in the towel as soon as their spouse sports spinach between his/her teeth, way before they even approach the concept of merger. Florie was one such person.

Early into her marriage, she discovered that her husband was not the guy she had dreamed of. PD (Passion Deprivation) set in soon after they had tied the knot. Before long, she was having one affair after another to bury her feelings of discontent and loneliness. Finally, three grown children and 30 years of marriage later, Florie was ready to call it quits.

YOUR CHEATER KEEPS CHEATING
—AND YOU'RE STILL THERE!

Perhaps it was the lump in her breast that scared Florie, or the high blood pressure she suddenly developed, or the big executive job she had just lost. Each of these alone would have been enough to terrify anyone, but all three together put Florie over the edge. Suddenly, the Band-Aid affairs she was able to apply over three decades were not sufficient. She was recognizing that her life as usual could not go on as it had.

Passion Deprivation generally follows our anthropological guidelines: heat often evaporates after a three-year hump. Three years was as long as Carmen Electra and Dave Navarro lasted. He said he loved her, but that the "connection was gone." In Touch Magazine quotes an insider who says that Angelina Jolie and Brad Pitt "always had a tempestuous relationship, and they appear to function best when the temperature is turned up high." But as the world has seen, such scorching heat cannot last. It's true that some couples sexualize their anger. But as Jude Law's Alfie character said in the movie by the same name, "We all have an expiration date."

In the expiring timeline under which we're pressed to perform, people are ready to bolt as soon as they realize that every day won't deliver a smiley face. So, they rush off somewhere else, to scratch whatever itch they think they have, wherever it may be, with little thought of consequences. Singles bed

CHAPTER 2

Cheataholics Are Not Motivated By Sex Alone

The cheataholic is not a sex addict. The cheataholic is usually not even a "player." The cheataholic is your average Jack or Jill who entered a committed union with the best of intentions. Acknowledging that the thrill is gone, this person is now terrified that s/he no longer has the wherewithal to return to the groove once enjoyed.

By the time they begin their transgression, cheataholics are so desperate to save themselves, they mindlessly put their own needs and desires above everyone else's—even to the point of engaging in unsavory activities.

♕
**Gilda-Gram®
The first time a cheataholic cheats
is never the last.**

   Cheataholics continue behaving in ways that will
further mar the relationship that might be worth
saving. While rationalizing their right to grab
gratification on the sly, they dismiss the
consequences, even when they might be devastating
or deadly! One married woman revealed she wanted
to cheat with a man she knew had herpes. An angry
gay man in a committed relationship said he didn't
care that the hot man on the side that he desired had
AIDS.

   Loving someone and mutually taking the needed
precautions despite their STD is one thing. But to be
caught by the person you're "committed" to because
that person contracted a disease you picked up from
a stranger is considered a crime. STD's and AIDS
aside, just one long French kiss exchanges more than
40,000 parasites and 250 types of bacteria! How
appetizing does that sound?

   People misconceive that it's only the partner left
behind who is in pain after a transgression. As R &
B songstress Rihanna belts out in her single,
"Unfaithful,"

*I don't wanna do this anymore.
I don't wanna be the reason why.*

YOUR CHEATER KEEPS CHEATING
—AND YOU'RE STILL THERE!

Every time I walk out the door,
I seem to die a little more inside.
I don't wanna hurt him anymore,
I don't wanna take away his life.
I don't want to be a murderer.

The question is never, "Should I or shouldn't I cheat?" Rather, it's, "Why do I have these urges?" People must painfully examine the time when things in their relationship began to slide. Then they must honestly discuss how their relationship was derailing. Few couples have the courage to slice open this excruciating wound. Cheating appears to be an easier way out. But that's only the appearance.

To dispel the dread and to salvage a battered ego, the cheataholic searches elsewhere to replace the lost excitement. The search for a new playmate may not even be conscious, but searching "elsewhere" inevitably hypes the fireworks that ultimately beckon someone new. So, after an unfaithful episode, when 65% of couples remain together nonetheless, the big question is why the betrayed and injured party doesn't just say, "Hasta la vista, cheater!"

Everyone blames the cheataholic. Of course, to the mate who's been cheated on, there is never justification for such disrespect. But cheataholics misguidedly are trying to recapture what they lost over time. While the cheating itself may temporarily blot out Passion Deprivation, cheaters are not happy campers. One emailer who signed his name, "Guilty Cheater," told me, "I think I'm addicted to meeting new women. It seems I have two sides to myself, and now I'm losing my mind." I name this malady "The Ecstasy of Admiration." But as you will see, the ecstasy lasts only so long . . .

Infidelity is exciting at the start because it crosses the line into illicit territory, and its uncertainty builds a sexual and/or an emotional swell—at least at first. But after the predictability factor sets in, and they're caught with their proverbial pants down, or they're exhausted from living a duplicitous life, or they discover that their paramour wants commitment, or their passion runs out of steam, most cheataholics come face to face with anger or depression.

When I asked a cheating client why he doesn't just leave his wife and marry his girlfriend of many years, he astutely remarked, "Because then my girlfriend would become my wife, and that would mean all the usual B.S. that comes with the title! I'd rather continue things as they are."

This man must have found his girlfriend dull already, because he was even cheating on her. He finally consulted with me when his playing field became too crowded, and he felt he could no longer juggle all his lovers.

When cheataholics recognize how unhappy they are, my email inbox overflows with desperate pleas for answers, help, and even requests for craftier philandering techniques. Some ask for believable rationales they can "sell" their partner if they're caught, while others can't understand why the liar they cheated with eventually turned tail and cheated on them! The truth is,

♛
Gilda-Gram®
If a cheater cheats WITH you,
the cheater will cheat ON you.

Telling a married cheataholic that he can only sleep with his wife is like telling a dog he can't chase cars. Actually, the same reasoning abounds: dogs chase cars they can't catch, and people sleep with partners they'll never marry. *It's the thrill of the hunt.* And as soon as that thrill is gone, it's onto Next!

Country Music artist, Trisha Yearwood, in her song, "Sweet Love," describes the hunt in these lyrics:

It ain't the gettin', it's the wishin';
It ain't the catchin', it's the fishin';
It ain't the heaven, it's the preachin';
It ain't the catchin', it's the reachin'.

For most cheataholics, winning their prey is tantamount to being told they are still desired. For them, the reward of such an ego-booster is immeasurable! Too bad it won't last.

manage the high quality relationship you have already enjoyed so it can continue.

Years ago, before Fox News Channel turned to all politics, I appeared on O'Reilly to discuss the case of a 39-year-old woman with a 17-year-marriage who had seduced a 16-year-old boy and even gave him a $40,000 Mercedes to reward his interest in her. While O'Reilly looked to pin this phenomenon of older women/teenage guys on outside forces, I said that the blame game only goes as far as "the devil made me do it" and "the refrigerator made me fat." This woman must take responsibility for what is going on in her life and her marriage, rather than camouflage her issues through acting out behaviors with minors, I told him.

Confronting your partner with your true feelings is a lot more difficult than having a roll in the sack with an impressionable and inappropriate source. The outlandishness of this sort of pairing significantly added to this married woman's excitement.

The initial cheating contact may masquerade as lots of libido, but some cheataholics never even consummate the relationship because sex matters less than the quest to reaffirm their worth. They mistakenly believe that new sparks of passion will resuscitate their dried up existence. But they are acting not on their love or on their thirst for a particular person; they are acting on their fears.

YOUR CHEATER KEEPS CHEATING
—AND YOU'RE STILL THERE!

While channel-surfing one morning, a TV screen popped up, listing the signs that tell you your pet is afraid: biting, scratching, pacing, barking, and urinating. At once, I thought of how similar people are to their pets in their reactions to fear. The show's host asked the veterinarian in the studio how to treat a pet's fears. The doctor said to put the animal in a nice, safe place. In people-talk, that place is LOVE.

Love is expressed through passion. As soon as the passion appears to be evaporating, many people become anxious—and act out in ways not too dissimilar from their pet's biting, scratching, pacing, and barking, in most cases, without the urinating.

The myth of the cheataholic is that his/her cheating will offer an escape ticket to happiness. In an episode on the famed TV series, Sopranos, after rambling about the boring state of family life of the people he knows, Tony's psychiatrist, Dr. Melfi, asks him if he's bored. He sighs. He's unable to answer. Then he responds, "I got shot in the pancreas and I recovered. No brain damage from the septic shock like everybody figured I'd have. You know my feelings. Every day is a gift." His psychiatrist icily stares at him without a reaction, prompting him to continue. He replies, "Well, what are you gonna do? It's the human condition."

We learn that boredom is one of the contributing factors to Tony's cheating ways, rationalized as being part of "the human condition." But through his therapy sessions, it's revealed that his mother didn't protect him from his father, so he is angry for having felt so unloved. He's also bored with his life and marriage, and he has been emotionally separating himself from his wife for many years. But because of the way his wife nursed him back to health after being shot, he feels he owes her.

So, Tony now tries to refrain from acting on his impulses to cheat. But as soon as he learns that his nephew has been scoring with the woman Tony turned down out of his newfound guilt, he again becomes angry. He feels one-upped in the competitive game of manhood. Dr. Melfi instructs, "You don't have to eat every dish of rigatoni. You don't have to f--- every female you meet." But Tony doesn't buy it. His family history and his need for control dictate otherwise.

Tony Soprano is the fictitious metaphor for a cheataholic who continues to search for love gone missing from childhood. Because his childhood issues were never sufficiently dealt with, he cheats again and again and again—forever without finding the love in craves.

As a viewer, I was disappointed that Dr. Melfi never made the connection between Tony's anger toward his mother and his serial cheating, for me, the obvious key to unlocking the mystery behind her patient's unhappiness. Then again, knowing and participating in the entertainment business as I do, if she had made that connection, would his on-screen therapy have been so moving?

While Tony is a made-up character, cheataholics in real life are personally miserable for continuing to seek loving rewards in other people. Based on the cheataholics and their hurt partners I counsel, it becomes obvious that slimy sneaking around is not all it's cracked up to be. Most often, a cheating woman fantasizes her new partner as her soul mate, while her cheating male partner perceives their affair as just an exciting adventure. These differences evolve into big disappointments for both down the line.

From the start, cheating is electrifying because it's uncertain and thrilling. It's especially riveting when the cheataholic makes his/her paramour a new pet project.

The New York Post, Page Six, July 28, 2006 – Music industry insiders are whispering about the real reason Prince split from his wife of 5 years, Testolini Nelson. "Prince has been spending an inordinate amount of time with his new protégé, Tamar," said our source. "He is trying to get her signed with a major label and has her doing the rounds. Everyone takes the meeting because of Prince, but she's just a pretty girl singing Prince songs. It is not very good. He hasn't found a taker, but he is smitten with her.

Actually, a person doesn't necessarily have to be outright cheating on a partner to derive the exhilaration of excitement. Some people derive stimulation at the office just from the thrill of flirting with a co-worker. Such "badness" is especially exciting if the company prohibits romantic fraternizing between employees. For sure, the thrill of the cover-up adds to the heat!

After a while, in every aspect of our lives, the dust eventually settles. There are no free rides. For cheaters, predictability sets in, along with the exhaustion from living a duplicitous life. If one of the two parties no longer wants to dance to the old tune, or even wants to push for more closeness, the cheataholic will have to finally come face-to-face with how unhappy and frightened s/he truly is. That's when growth can occur—but it's also when fear might become paralyzing.

Judy came to me for an advice session. At 57, she had married her college professor who was 17 years her senior. After flirting with him, sleeping with him, and marrying him, she decided that the thrill of the get was gone. After 10 years of marriage, she found a married guy with whom she began cheating for the next 15 years.

YOUR CHEATER KEEPS CHEATING
—AND YOU'RE STILL THERE!

All was as exciting as any affair is—until his wife contracted a brain tumor. Suddenly, Judy was faced with her lover's guilt over leaving the wife who desperately needed him as her caretaker. To make matters more complex, Judy's own husband began to exhibit signs of dementia, and she began to see her life mirroring that of her 15-year paramour: taking care of the spouse who whom they were committed, coupled with the guilt for not having been there emotionally all those years.

Judy was now very anxious. Having just floated for a decade and a half through ecstatic interludes with her lover, reality was suddenly settling in. I told her this could be a time for her to grow. She begrudgingly agreed.

Sometimes a cheater intent on deceiving ends up having to pay an exorbitant sum of money, far more than s/he ever bargained for. A judge ruled that a woman who discovered her fiancé was married was able to keep her $40,000 engagement ring, even though she was the one who broke off the relationship. The man claimed he was in the midst of divorce. The woman also found that he had been trolling for women on the Internet. Although the man sued the woman to return either the ring or the $40,000 it cost him, the judge ruled otherwise. Luckily, this woman did her homework to prevent her courtship from becoming a future marital battleship.

enjoy a lifetime of wild, continuous passion, which is a major step beyond the drab and lonely life they knew before they were pierced by cupid. It's mostly women who read the romance novels that make this promise. And these female readers make this genre the best selling in the United States.

Proof of the genre's popularity is abundantly clear with the runaway lascivious best seller, "Fifty Shades of Grey," by E L James, followed by movies by the same name. Yet, most men, too, without needing to read these romantic fantasies, believe their life will be enhanced with a special partner.

However, something happens between the breathless "I love you" at the start of romance and the mythical swoons of "happily ever after" that follow. One real life story after another details how once-loving partners betray each other and violate their original intentions, promises, and vows. The Wall Street Journal calls infidelity "one of the biggest risks in marriage."

One of America's most renowned reality programming families, the Kardashians, generate headlines each time they have another cheating fiasco. Starting with their matriarch, in her 2011 memoir, Kris Jenner admitted to having an extra-marital affair with Todd Waterman while she was married to husband Robert Kardashian. Daughter

Chapter 1

Plentiful Inducements

According to evolutionary psychologists, fidelity is unnatural, and the ONLY creature that does not cheat is the flatworm. (So next time you call someone a "worm," know what you're really saying!) Each day, it seems, the news supports these claims with another straying spouse. Remember when it was Yankee superstar Alex Rodriguez (A-Rod), married for five years? In the same week, it was Los Angeles Mayor, Antonio Villaraigosa, married for 20 years. (He must have adored his wife at one time because he joined his last name with hers when they wed.) Within the same time span, it was the Mayor of Detroit, with his faithful wife sitting beside him, as he apologized to her, to his family, and to his constituents for having an affair with a staff member—and lying about it. What happened to these and countless other marriages gone bad? What became of that accepted promise of fidelity?

song's words, a relationship "don't mean a thing if it ain't got that zing!" To be in a state of continuous "zing," then, the cheataholic may be addicted to stray with one partner or many—to assure the continuation of the heat, but also to assure him/herself that s/he's still got what it takes!

Chimpanzees are known to have sex 20 or more times a day. While this would be a stretch for human beings, the desire for endless passion in people new to a relationship seems just as insatiable at first. However, anthropologists in the past dampened that quest by noting this semi-psychotic, walk-into-walls brand of ecstasy could last *no more than three years*. It was thought to be one of those unfortunate blink-and-you'll-miss-it facts of life. Newer findings debunk the myth that passion ends. Sure, it becomes more comfortable and settled, but it can still be as hot as it once was.

Many committed people choose cheating as an easy way to cope with what I call PD: Passion Deprivation. Even those you might never suspect to stray fall into this trap. The Hebrew University in Jerusalem unsealed letters that shed new light on the personal life of the 20th century's greatest intellect, Albert Einstein. While most folks thought the geeky guy with the unruly hair was solely into his E=MC2 discovery, it was revealed that Einstein had 10 lovers, in addition to the two women he married!

down together soon after saying "hello," and, with apologies to Michaelangelo, they part almost after their first supper. For couples that have made it to formal commitment, the original passion that brought them to this state seems to quickly die amid dullness.

Mary and John, both 26 years old, had been married for four years. During that time, they split, re-united, split, re-united, and split again. Finally, they both began to see other people. However, Mary contacted me to begin work on herself, in hopes of reconciling with John. I could not give her hope of a definite future with her husband, but I told her that her idea of working on herself was a good one, at least to unravel some of the problems she and John had had.

Like so many relationships we know, this pair continued their on-again, off-again dance, which kept their excitement pumped. Sometimes, deliberately devised on-off periods keep titillation running longer than a relationship's expected longevity. Although it is a common joke, the real reason make-up sex is mind-blowing is because it recaptures the original state of new passion—and new passion can never compete with the crusty, routine version.

Chapter 3

All Systems Need Maintenance

All systems break down without maintenance. Recently, on the TV show for Investigation Discovery, "50 Ways to Leave Your Lover," I reiterated, "Eventually, even the best lubed parts need to be taken out for service." Your car will malfunction unless you maintain it, and your body will crash unless you sustain it. The same exists with relationships. Clearly, they, too, must be *worked*.

I name the skill required to support a relationship over time, "Relationship Management." I teach courses in "Business Management." And companies advertise their fabulous service as, "Customer Relationship Management." Whether it's relationship management, business management, or customer relationship management, the demand is to

Chapter 4

Cheaters Cheat Because They Think They Can

Early one morning in New York, I received calls from In Touch Magazine, People, Entertainment Tonight, Access Hollywood, Vogue Brazil, Cosmo Taiwan, Elle Hong Kong and tons of other media outlets throughout the world. Since I'm a recognizable media personality, this is nothing new in any typical day. However, on this day, unbeknownst to me, the following piece had been written in The Sunday Express, a British publication:

> *Sunday Express, Sienna Miller Seeks Shrink Over Law's 'Cheataholism'!, August 8, 2005, Hollywood actress Sienna Miller has reportedly sought advice from a top relationship psychotherapist over her wrecked relationship with estranged fiancé Jude Law.*

YOUR CHEATER KEEPS CHEATING
—AND YOU'RE STILL THERE!

According to sources, Miller has consulted New York academic Dr. Gilda Carle over her lover's affair with his children's nanny Daisy Wright, and wants to find out reasons behind his infidelity.

Dr. Gilda has been talking to Sienna about what she has coined the 'cheataholic' and examining the causes for rampant infidelity," a source told the Sunday Express.

My initial response to this story was shock. I would never discuss who seeks counsel from me, or whom I service. Even my unsolicited Testimonials on my web site, DrGilda.com, which include real names of real people, are posted only after I have been granted permission from the writers. So where did this leak come from?? The Brits even knew enough to call me an "academic," and I was indeed a college professor, so they obviously did their research.

About 75% of my clientele consists of high profile people, but never before has anything so revealing about any possible (or impossible) clients hit the press. While I'm forever interviewed about the behaviors of celebrities for tabloids, magazines, and entertainment shows, I never discuss whom I treat or who I know.

By the next day, the Jude Law/Sienna Miller story hit Page Six of the New York Post, the most revered gossip column in the world. That night, I clocked thousands of hits to my web site. Despite all the questions posed to me, I would not confirm or deny an association with Sienna Miller, or any other of my clients. Reporters tried to get me to say that Jude Law was a sex addict. Of course, I wouldn't comment on that either.

I told the media that since I would not speak about the validity of their information, I didn't think this was even a story of interest to them. But the news was hitting papers from New York to India, with vast geography in between. Usually, such tabloid pieces evaporate after a day, quickly becoming old news. But this story had legs. It actually took a full week of gossip chaos for me to finally get my life back—in part. I was interviewed about cheating by magazines from around the world, including Elle Hong Kong, and Cosmopolitan China, as you can see here:

用出轨报复出轨
来源：《时尚·Cosmopolitan》2005年11月号
　　文/杨倩莹
　　报复只会造成恶性循环
有些女性虽然不会自杀，不过会以报复作为反击。
　　对于这种反应，Dr. Gilda提出警告："报复只会让你得到10秒钟的满足感，之后你会为自己的行为后悔不已。因为生理的构造不同，男人可以有空洞的性爱，但是女人　却不能。而且这也只会造成恶性循环。"

　　　Dr. Gilda的一位女客户在发现她的老公有外遇之后，气愤地对她说："我要让我的老公尝到这种生不如死的感觉，我要报复。"尽管Dr. Gilda建议她不要如此冲动，但是这位女客户还是跑到酒吧来了个一夜情，隔天理直气壮地向老公炫耀。

　"她不但把老公给气个半死，结果自己也后悔不已。她的老公完全没有办法接受老婆和别的男人上床，觉得自己的男性尊严完全扫地，两个人到现在还在不断地接受心理咨询。"

冷静情绪，对症下药

Dr. Gilda说，外遇有时像是一棒惊醒梦中人，让你痛定思痛，好好思索自己在两人之间所扮演的角色为何。在泪水流干之后，你可以暂时不和爱人见面或是讲电话，也不要急着找寻下一个真命天子，而是应该好好冷静下来。

　"每一件事情都不是偶然发生的，事情发生都是有原因的。虽然你会觉得很心痛，但是外遇却是一个讯息，让你知道二人之间的关系需要修复。你必需好好想一想找出事出的原因，惟有这样事情才不会再重复发生。"

婚变事件后的珍妮弗·安妮斯顿也对《Vanity Fair》表示："我想这个时候最好还是一个人，这会使你重新发掘自己并且进入另一个领域。如果你可以从不同的角度去看杯子是半满时，那就是你学习最多的时候。"她并且透露她的心理治疗师给她的金玉良言:"就算是有**98％**是对方的**错**,那么也有 **2％**是你的**错**,这百分之二就是就是我们要对症下**药**的。"

　　Dr.Gilda表示,不管对方是不是要**继续这**段感情,当你觉得自己情**绪**比**较稳**定时,你可以和**爱**人见面或是通过**电话讨论**是什么原因使他有外遇。"逃避不是解决问**题**的最佳方法,因为如果你不对症下**药**,同样的问**题**下次可能会再次**发**生。"

Of course, I was only able to decipher all the Dr. Gildas throughout the story. But obviously, cheating is fascinating business to audiences near and far.

Years ago, In Touch Magazine ran a poll of their readers who answered the burning question of whether they thought Jessica Simpson cheated on her then husband, Nick Lachey. Sixty-one percent said, "Yes." As part of the poll the magazine's research quoted a statistic that only 35% of American marriages survive an affair. I don't know how the survey defined "survive." In my work with clients, sometimes a person finds it impossible to forget the image of his/her mate in bed with someone else, and they can't get past the hurt and humiliation.

Just one week after the Sienna Miller/Jude Law fiasco, something seemingly coincidental occurred. As the "30-Second Therapist" for the TODAY Show and the "Ask Dr. Gilda" advice columnist for

YOUR CHEATER KEEPS CHEATING
—AND YOU'RE STILL THERE!

Match.com, I was always responding to different lifestyle and relationship questions. One week, someone wrote to me about loving a "Bad Boy," and my Social Media accounts spiked again. Another week, the title of a reader's question was, "I Fell for a Married Man." This one attracted so much traffic in one day, my website's server crashed!

My book sales were going through the roof. When MSN.com ran one of these columns on their main page, the same thing occurred. Still another week, I answered a question titled, "I Fell for My Best Friend's Ex," and it attracted more huge numbers of followers and likes. While not a typical cheating story, the scope of this question considered who's dateable, who's off limits, and what behavior crosses the line.

On its home page, Yahoo.com repeated my column about dating a married man. Again, my Social Media went nuts. The subject of cheating draws huge interest. I receive emails from those who admit to cheating and from partners who are betrayed. The cheaters seek rationalizations for their actions, and their cuckolded partners want remedies for their mates to reform! I wrote this book to make some sense out of the crushing pain so many people are feeling when they're somehow part of a cheating duo.

Chapter 5

My Friend's Cheating Husband

I set up a lunch date with my friend, Ellen, who I
had not seen in about two years. I was delighted to
finally catch up with her for some heart-to-heart girl
talk. But when I arrived at the restaurant, she
announced, "I hope you don't mind. Fred [her
husband] will be joining us." "How surprising," I
thought. "We're getting together for the first time in
years, and she's bringing her husband along?"

But our lunch was wonderfully pleasant, and I
enjoyed seeing both of them, and catching up on
things going on in our community. A week later, I
called Ellen to say how terrific it was to see her, and
that we ought to get together again sometime soon
for the girl talk we had originally planned.

Now able to speak candidly, my friend launched
into a lengthy story about how she had caught her
very conservative, physicist husband, Fred, cheating

with a girl he sought out from his kindergarten class (!!), who was now an aggressive AND ALSO MARRIED surgeon. The idea of Ellen's husband cheating was a hard image for me to conjure up. This guy seemed to be anything but the type who looked like a cheater—whatever that's supposed to mean.

After 20 years of marriage to my friend, with three daughters who graduated from Ivy League colleges, he appeared to be a dedicated scientist, an intellectual snob, an endless researcher always seeking more findings that would help his field, and an introverted, asocial guy who was strictly into his work. After she discovered the news, Ellen detailed how she cried every day to her children and her female friends and even to her clients. With her adult friends, she learned that one by one, each of them offered up a story of how *her* husband had cheated, too.

At the end of our telephone talk, Ellen sighed, "So when Fred asked to join you and me for lunch, I was delighted that he even wants to spend time with me these days." I thought, "*He* cheated on *her*, and she's feeling insecure?"

I saw Ellen for lunch again three weeks later, and this time, it was just the two of us. I told her how disturbed I had been about her news. She expanded on the history of her marriage. She said, "Fred has always been fascinated by successful, brilliant women with advanced degrees. When I was eight months pregnant, he became 'friendly' with another physicist who had just discovered a new theory. Some years later, I discovered that he had befriended a very talented, intensely competitive cosmetic dentist at his hospital."

I responded, "Maybe Fred never really physically cheated. Maybe he was an emotional cheater throughout your marriage." Ellen agreed. Amazingly, Fred displayed all the traits of a cheataholic.

As I listened to my friend's story, I recognized that during each of her husband's distractions, Ellen would review her own adequacy. As a result of this latest and real physical affair, Ellen even apologetically told Fred, "I feel I pulled a bait and switch on you when we first fell in love. I had told you that I planned to go to grad school. But when we started to discuss our plans for children and a solid family life, I changed my career goals to accommodate our new needs. Maybe I have never accomplished enough for you."

Ellen suffered self-loathing and self-blame. Why did she take on all the ills of her marriage as though they were her sole responsibility? Most women think of themselves as the "relationship police," totally to blame for all the issues that don't work in their romance.

During our lunch, Ellen now described Fred's
latest female "friend," a prominent heart surgeon.
He had excitedly described her to Ellen, and said that
she and her husband were meeting him for coffee
that afternoon. He didn't invite Ellen. But she was
now on to him, his attractions, and his distractions,
and she warned that if he took his latest flirtation any
further, she'd leave.

Once a woman who didn't even know how to turn
on a computer, now Ellen decoded her husband's
computer password (!!), and was committing high
tech surveillance on all his emails.

"What a way to live," I thought. Yet, when I
suggested that perhaps the two of them would
eventually pursue separate paths, Ellen emphatically
said, "No, that's never going to happen. After all
these years, of course we'll still be together." So, it
was clear: even if Ellen needed to nail Jell-O to a
tree, as set up and fed up as she might have felt,
she'd stick with Fred, no matter what he did and with
whom he cavorted.

♛

Gilda-Gram®
A behavior only continues for as long
as it provides a payoff.

Ellen's pain was obviously not as great as her payoffs:

1. the material affects that symbolized to the world that she was loved *lavishly*, and

2. the security of knowing she had someone she could call her "husband."

Ellen enjoyed her luxuries, her husband, Fred, was never satisfied with anything he had, and forever desired MORE. Perhaps it was because he never felt truly accepted by his parents when he was growing up. Perhaps it was because his critical folks continued to question his earnings, even now, as a middle-aged and very successful professional man. So, at 48 years old, he aimed to prove on the outside that he was MORE THAN what he felt he was inside.

Fred suddenly sported a bright red Jaguar, he changed his traditional buttoned-down shirts to flamboyant casual wear, he was dousing himself with sickeningly sweet cologne, and he started feigning a lack of time to accompany Ellen to the activities he had customarily shared with her and once seemingly enjoyed. Not surprisingly, she discovered that he had plenty of time to accompany his new female "friends" to their special events.

Apparently, like many other people in our culture, and particularly a man initiated into mid-life, Fred suffered from what I've named the "Never Enough"

Syndrome. People afflicted with this malady feel empty, no matter what they've accomplished, where they live, and how many "toys" they've amassed. These people suffer from what experts describe as the "Imposter Phenomenon," believing they don't deserve what they have earned, and they don't measure up to expectations either they or others have placed on them.

Ellen's husband had two Ph.D.s and a huge, responsible job as a brainiac at a think tank. They lived in a beautiful home with an indoor swimming pool, sauna, and horses in the backyard, in a very prestigious town. Ellen worked two part time jobs until she decided to devote her entire professional life to her personal fitness training. She was making a comfortable living to add to that of her husband's. She was in exceptional shape for a woman in her late 40s, and she wanted for absolutely nothing material. The kids were grown and living on their own. Whenever a new and improved exercise machine appeared on the market, although the couple already had an older model with a few less bells and whistles, they upgraded. When Ellen tired of her old car, although she hardly drove it, she wrote a check for a new one.

To the outside world, this pair had it all. But Fred's inner demons caused him to feel emotionally bankrupt—and Ellen apologized for not giving him what he needed. Rather than stand her ground and take pride in all she had personally accomplished, Ellen followed Fred's lead to question what she could do to make him love and accept her more.

Based on the Jude Law/Sienna Miller fiasco on which I had been quoted throughout the world, with the hundreds of emails I received about cheaters who were miserable, and now, the situation in Ellen's life, I began to question the sanctity of every relationship I knew, casually and intimately.

Chapter 6

Are You In A Courtship Or On A Battleship?

One of my single girlfriends had been living with a man for three years, but she confided that their relationship was not working out. She said she asked him to move out, but he resisted, and the two of them continued the game of playing house. Obviously, they were both deriving payoffs great enough to keep them bound together for at least this amount of time.

But my friend revealed they were no longer having sex because she rejected his "slam, bam, thank-you, m'am" lovemaking. "Did you discuss this with him?" I asked. She said she didn't want to. *Talk about suppressed anger!*

My friend's style of communication was to withhold intimacy from him, while she stuffed her anger into her body, becoming fatter and fatter. When I visited and saw them together, I noticed how solicitous he was of her, desperately trying to please her in every way he could. But she responded with icy coldness.

As I had suspected, she admitted that some therapy sessions revealed her anger at life in general. I asked, "What are you going to do about it?" "Well," she said, "Mel said that since I rejected him sexually, he would like to sleep with other women." But she told him, "Wherever you sleep is where you can stay." So, in effect, she ordered, "You can't sleep with me, but you can't cheat on me, either."

Another guy might have fled, but this guy stayed put, sleeping in my friend's bed, sharing her life, and following her lead as a compliant partner. I wondered what his payoff was. But I already knew. She was a media star, and he was a hapless job drifter who loved attending his gal pal's high profile events. He was willing to exchange the glare of the limelight for the dimness of the sensual shadows in which he dwelled.

As for my friend, having never married, and having never felt totally loved, she was willing to keep up an appearance of having someone who cared. Great payoffs with vacant passions—but each derived enough to keep the myth continue to afloat.

YOUR CHEATER KEEPS CHEATING
—AND YOU'RE STILL THERE!

Despite protestations, abuse, poor treatment, and apathy, many people remain coupled because they are too frightened to be on their own, and terrified that they might have to admit they are unlovable. So, they remain—and complain. My friend is not the only one who stays, although she's unhappily married.

> _The New York Post_, _Cindy Adams, October 4, 2005 -- The social Kempners, Tommy the banker and Park Avenue Princess Nan, were married over 50 years. Slim, soignée, best-dressed Nan Kempner left us so recently that her memorial was barely a week ago. He's already planning to get married. Already. If the man's picked the organist and calligrapher yet, this I don't know. That everyone's whispering how he's looking toward this milestone, this I know. Their "open" marriage was not closed information. At one of last year's innumerable society balls, a friend — fretting over Nan's health — asked, "Are you all right? You happy?"_

> _Watching her husband dancing with this certain lady, she replied: "How happy can I be when he's hugging his mistress?"_

Nan Kempner died of emphysema, a disease described by metaphysical healer, Louise Hay, as a "fear of taking in life. Not worthy of living." Like my friend, Ellen, the fear of losing the security she thought she possessed kept Mrs. Kempner in a terribly painful marriage. As the noted psychologist Abraham Maslow said, "One can choose to go back toward safety or forward toward growth. Growth must be chosen again and again; fear must be overcome again and again."

I didn't know this woman, but Cindy Adams' description of her unhappiness seemed devastating, as she stood helplessly by, watching her husband slip away into the arms of someone else. The thousands of emails I receive share the sadness and pain both from the one cheated on, as well as from the cheater who continues to seek some solace, somewhere.

After my friend's shocking revelation, I was invited to Ellen and Fred's house one evening for a family dinner. As I looked around the table at the 10 people sitting there, I noticed that Fred's eyes looked vacant. He said little, he obediently helped serve the food and clean the dishes, but he appeared to be far off somewhere else. As the chatter and laughter sprinkled the party, it seemed that I was the only one who recognized his emotional absence.

I guess it didn't really matter; Ellen said that she was dedicated to this marriage for the long haul, no matter what. These were two people living under the same opulent roof, going through the steps of their different exotic dances, but adorning masks preventing anyone from possibly knowing the truth that they covered.

YOUR CHEATER KEEPS CHEATING
—AND YOU'RE STILL THERE!

During dessert, I discovered that I was wrong about one of my suppositions. There was at least one other person at this dinner party who sensed this couple's discontent: one of their daughters who was 22 years old. In a casual discussion we were having about how she's been, what she's doing, and where she's going, she openly shared that despite loving and living with her boyfriend, she had chosen never to get married.

When I asked her why, her matter-of-fact response surprised me, "There's too much cheating." So, there it was. Ellen and Fred were unwittingly passing their distrust for one another down to the genes of the next generation. I thought, "This girl is too young to be such a pessimist! What a shame."

As time went on, I began to listen to people's cheating revelations with a more discerning eye. A wealthy 63-year-old businessman I vaguely knew at my gym, without provocation, openly spilled his story during my workouts on the exercise machines. He said that after his "catting around" for decades, his wife of 38 years had just moved out and was in therapy. She said she needed "time to heal."

As we paced our side-by-side treadmills, he complained about having to pay double overhead, two mortgages, plus he was supporting his son and his kids through a divorce. The loud-mouthed braggadocio boasted multiple high-end cars, boats, an airplane, and a rich life style. But now he was bemoaning multiple physical ailments, one of which involved sharp pains in his testicles.

I'm a believer that the diseases we take on reflect the kinds of issues we need to resolve. Testicular pain may or may not reflect issues down below, but it's geographically close enough to ponder as just desserts for a cheating man. The man revealed that over the years, as he traveled across the country to build his now very successful business, he was pursued by one attractive woman after another. He justified his cheating by saying that his very religious wife refused to have sex with the lights on. The contrasts between this man's conservative wife and the quick-to-disrobe women who pursued him were great. Over the years, as his wealth increased, so did his straying.

Now he complained that since his wife discovered his extracurricular indulgences, he had not had sex in over a year. Perhaps that's why his testicles ached! To add salt to his wound, he said that his buddies, all of whom sported women on the side, were shocked that he had gotten caught, while they were able to successfully get away with their philandering.

♛

Gilda-Gram®
The probability of being caught is
directly proportional to the riskiness of the act.

YOUR CHEATER KEEPS CHEATING
—AND YOU'RE STILL THERE!

The remarks from this guy's friends focused not on cheating in and of itself, or on how their own actions affected their wives, but on the improbability of them being caught red-handed.

"How could your wife have found out? How could she know all the names of the women, when the flowers were delivered, the cost of the hotel bills, and the length of the telephone calls? Aren't there laws of privacy? Get a lawyer, man!" they vehemently advised him.

As I treadmilled faster and faster to distance myself from the gory details I wanted to forget, the man sighed that if he had it to do all over, he'd never cheat with anyone again. Typical of most cheataholics who are caught, now this guy said that he was feeling sick, he missed his wife, he hated living alone, and he was frustrated that she wasn't jumping back into their home and marriage, as the dependent woman he thought he had married. His was just one of many tales of infidelity that were pouring at me at this time.

While these stories may appear to be simple tales of people looking for meaning outside their marriages, little do they recognize how dangerous this behavior can be. Newsweek Magazine warned that many of the world's women erroneously believe that marriage is a protection from sexually transmitted diseases such as AIDS. Unfortunately, they later discover that because of their husbands' philandering, they are being put at risk. A whopping 80% of women newly infected with HIV think they are practicing monogamy within their marriage or long-term union. The receptive nature of a woman's physiology makes her twice as prone as a man to contract HIV from a partner. How does a spouse explain a gift like that?

Anna Benson, married for seven years to Kris Benson, ex-Mets pitcher who moved to the Baltimore Orioles, filed for divorce after she caught her husband cheating. She called cheating on the ball field "sort of an epidemic. I blame the players. I don't blame anybody else."

After she publicly threatened to sleep with everyone on his ball team if she ever caught her husband in such an indelicate situation, she said, "I'm not saying I wouldn't forgive my husband. It would greatly depend on the situation, because that's what marriage is about." She dismissed her divorce petition a few days after she filed it.

Few romantic replacements can compete with a ballplayer's salary and lifestyle payoffs. People without such incentives often have a different view.

Simple Southern Gentleman emailed me that he would have been happy with just one wife and a few kids. But as a result of both his first and second wife cheating on him, he was now a Complicated Southern Gentleman with a history of three wives, six children, and three grandkids, all of whom vie for his attention and affection—which stresses him out. He signed his email, "Think I Got It Right Now." I hope he finally did!

Like Anna Benson, one of my clients also called cheating an epidemic. It not only affects the adults involved, but their offspring, as well. Yet the temptation of crossing the boundary into forbidden territory continues to tantalize the transgressors as well as their rubberneckers. The difference between the folks who act out their cheataholic temptations and those who get vicarious thrills from watching them is the difference between impetuous kids who can't differentiate between fantasy and reality, and grown-ups who can—and do.

The thought that a person's sexual power is not as great as it could be, or even as strong as it was long ago, is extremely distressing. Country Music singer, Toby Keith, pokes fun at this reality in his song, "As Good As I Once Was":

I ain't as good as I once was,
but I'm as good once as I ever was.

Nonetheless, our culture pressures people to maintain their wetness and wildness. For most, it's less about the technical mechanics of sex, and more about feeling continuously admired, respected, caressed, and loved.

In a survey by KSL Resorts, it was found that more men have begun hitting the spas lately, and 62% of them want to be massaged more than anything else. The skin is a human's largest organ, and the need for touch is extraordinary, particularly if it is missing at home. But even if people are deriving a good deal of attention and love on the home front, do they think whatever they're getting is adequate? Like my friend Ellen's husband, many young and healthy people in the prime of their lives continue to sport of feeling that no amount is ever enough.

Chapter 7

The Mighty Fantasy Brain

A pig's orgasm lasts a full 30 minutes, which is a seemingly similar desire of young, healthy college men at the prime of their lives. Children's Memorial Hospital and Northwestern University's Feinberg School of Medicine, both in Chicago, studied 234 sexually active men, 18 to 25 years old. They found that 13% of the men said they'd experienced erectile dysfunction, but rarely discussed this with a doctor.

Erectile dysfunction, or impotence, was defined as *ever* having difficulty getting or keeping an erection—which is normal occasionally for any man. Think of the expectations that have been set for male sexual performance. Perhaps it's no accident that every episode of Seinfeld contains a Superman reference by name or picture somewhere in at least one scene—which Jerry Seinfeld even extended to his commercials with American Express. The

Seinfeld show has become such a cultural icon, the Superman expectation may have been taken too literally by young men.

Twenty-five percent of the men in the Chicago study said they lost an erection while putting on a condom. So, they were four times less likely to use condoms consistently. Most of the students mixed Viagra, Cialis or Levitra with alcohol, methamphetamines, cocaine and ecstasy. Unfortunately, Viagra won't transform Average Joe into Sperm Man, but he is probably likely to have more sex over shorter periods of time. In a Quebec study, when male rats were given alcohol, they attempted sex with females who had just rejected them. It was found that under the influence, anything goes to keep passion flowing.

Yet, prolonged erections can cause brain damage among men. Therefore, is raising the bar worth any of the consequences? While I get just a few questions from emailers regarding specific sexual techniques, the bulk of my mail concerns the sustainability of people's relationships.

When I began my writing and my practice, my fans were mostly women and teenage girls. These days, that demographic has expanded to include men and teenage boys. One email after another begs for remedies for lasting love. As Hollywood heartthrob, Vince Chase, in the fictitious HBO series, Entourage, found in an episode, when his ex-lover,

YOUR CHEATER KEEPS CHEATING
—AND YOU'RE STILL THERE!

Mandy Moore, flung her arrow into his heart, not even the multimillion-dollar action movie he was filming could absorb his pain. Women have a tough time accepting this, but when love goes sour, men hurt, too.

It's not just young American men who want to bump up their virility. In India's New Delhi, an 88-year-old man fathered a child and attributed the secret of his sexual prowess to camel milk. While doctors say there is no scientific basis for the claim, thousands of men clamored for the drink, and sales of camel milk shot up, with dealers doubling their prices.

Men young and old across all reaches of the world want to sustain their passion, and they're willing to try whatever new remedy comes to market. Actually, maybe a man's desire to get all he can as soon and as often as he can has merit; a study at the University of Pennsylvania showed that men's brains deteriorate faster than woman's brains—so they'd better hurry up!

As a guest on the TODAY Show, I was asked to discuss "Wall Street Brokers Who Frequent Strip Clubs—and How It Affects Their Relationships at Home." I fielded email questions from female viewers, many of who were steamed that their marriages or supposedly committed relationships had exploded after their men engaged in this behavior.

Some women accepted their men's club-hopping as not important to argue over, others put up with it to keep peace at home, and still others accompanied their guys on their visits to lend a watchful (and distrusting) eye over what was going on.

Strip clubs may have become even more legitimized because the fictitious Tony Soprano owned the Bada Bing. But they are also seen as a rite of passage: England's Prince Harry made news for going to one to celebrate the end of his army officer training. Yet, to err on the side of the conservative convention, the media were quick to note that the third in line to the British throne turned down a lap dance when one was offered. (He didn't stick to that conviction in later years when he was caught stripped naked at a rambunctious party, and the photos surfaced worldwide!) Now he and his wife, Meagan Markle can have a good laugh at the silly antics of a young prince who was anxious to grow up.

In hypocritical America, strip clubs play a part of the Wall Street fabric as a form of legal sexual rubbernecking. To add insult to injury to the angry and aggrieved women at home, the IRS allows this to be a legitimate deductible expense, loosely considered a form of "business meeting."

This is an explosive topic that seems to peak huge interest. Even before appearing on the TODAY Show with this topic, I received many emails about

husbands' prying eyes, from wives who felt
threatened. One woman who discovered her
husband's predilection for porn sites on the web said
she felt "physically ill" after her discovery. While
she said she prided herself on feeling well balanced
and mature, she admitted she lost her self-esteem,
especially after she "lowered herself" to taking nude
pictures of herself to make her man happy and keep
him faithful. She blamed his obsession on her own
shortcomings, imagining that she could never meet
the physical standards her husband enjoyed watching
in his fantasy world.

Yale researchers found that people with low self-
esteem tend to see their partners as either all good or
all bad. Consequently, they struggle with the
conflicting feelings of whether to remain in their
relationship or to withdraw loving feelings in an
attempt at self-protection. Self-protection is a reason
people set up walls between themselves and others,
and even why they might obsess over their
appearance, which they deem to be not up to par:
"I'm so unattractive, no one would ever love me, so I
might as well not even try to find love."

Imagined ugliness is called "body dysmorphic
disorder." It is worrisome for me to receive emails
where the partner of a porn-purveyor internalizes it
as her fault. Studies show that people who suffer
from this disorder are 45 times more likely to

commit suicide than people in the general population.

Men are naturally curious when it comes to seeing naked women. Some women are just as curious about seeing naked men, but not to the extent that men believe they are when they sext someone they barely know. Then, there's a difference between an occasional glance and out-and-out preoccupation to the exclusion of your relationship at home. When a partner's interest begins with porn and extends into taking lovers on the side, the marriage is in serious trouble.

To prevent that from happening in their own marriage, some women try to accommodate their men by posing and posturing seductively, selfie style, for their husbands. But they should know that's not the answer to keep their guy, because their husband's draw is the thrill of the unknown. It is the fantasy of the unobtainable bodies that is at the heart of what beckons.

Women in pain need to reveal their true feelings to their men, rather than twist themselves inside out to resemble their guys' fantasy women. And then these women need to listen to their men about their feelings regarding their relationship.

Opening this sort of discussion is scary, because you never know what will be revealed, and what will hurt so deeply. But communication is at the heart of understanding.

♛

Gilda-Gram®
Understanding is what determines
the health and longevity of every union.

I sent the transcript of the TODAY Show to some people on my mailing list. One of my college students who has heard me rant about the necessity for people to "Live the Capital 'I' Life," as I call it, said, "This topic really hit home. My boyfriend just went to Las Vegas for a bachelor party and I knew that they would end up hitting a few strip clubs. Thank you for your comments. You always make us feel better about ourselves."

Page Six once revealed that Lindsay Lohan was "glued" to her new flavor of the minute, Harry Morton. During the same year, Lindsay had also entertained romances with Joaquin Phoenix, Sean Lennon, Jared Leto, Wilmer Valderrama, Brett Ratner, Johnny Knoxville, and Diana Ross' son, Evan, among others. Today, her list of romantic interests is many miles longer. It was rumored she was addicted to love. At the time, the tabloid wrote that "she flips out if any other girl is around" Morton. She constantly texts, emails, and calls him.

A year later, Lohan was trying to glue herself to Spider-Man star, James Franco, who rebuffed her. If we follow her pattern to this moment, we see a beautiful and talented actress who has continued throughout her years to enact the same dysfunctional behaviors, while trying to grab for love. Grabbing is a turn-off to any likely prospect, and she remains alone, looking worn.

With this backdrop, I questioned my student's feelings about her boyfriend's visit. She replied, "Well, as you know, I am pretty secure with myself. (Yes, over the course of several semesters, I noted her glowing self-confidence.) I have been with my guy for four years now and our relationship is solid. We are honest with each other and I really believe that is what keeps us together." She was so right!

♛

Gilda-Gram®
You can be either honest or dishonest.
There's no in-between.

My student continued, "I know that this was a weekend away with a very good friend before his wedding, and if a visit to a strip club was going to break us as a couple, it could have happened right here in New York. Of course, I questioned how he behaved without me there, but then I realized that I needed to live my life. So, I got together with my girls, and had a great weekend."

She continued "I felt better knowing that we were both with our friends, enjoying separate activities. The funny thing was that he called me more times than I could count, just to say, 'I love you,' or to see how I was. For most women, strip clubs are out of the question, but I have been to a few with my guy friends and I went to one with my boyfriend. I think that if a woman is secure with herself, she can compete with anything. I learned a lot about the clientele and the girls themselves. Actually, they should all have a chance to spend time with you, Dr. Gilda. Ha! What a compelling reality show 'Dr. Gilda and the Strippers' would make!"

A friend of mine who was hosting male businessmen from Europe as part of her corporate role said that her foreign visitors thought the American media's attention to this story about strippers was ridiculous. I suggested that in Europe, cheating is openly sanctioned as part of the culture, whereas in the United States, grabbing a glance at porn, or visiting a nudey bar and getting lap dances are guilty pleasures camouflaged beneath expensive business suits.

While one culture is more honest about satisfying their cravings than the other is, no matter where people live, few understand what really comprises a healthy relationship, and what is required to sustain its longevity.

Chapter 8

Like Sex, Commitment Used To Last Longer

As relationship challenged as this world seems to get, the wedding industry continues to grow. Yet, the institution of marriage is constantly being derided by both genders. One anonymous commenter on the Internet snarled, "Many of my married male friends sound more like hostages than husbands."

People appear to have a love/hate relationship with long-term commitment. They tend to express their disappointment about their own circumstances, yet no matter how bad things may be for them, the longing to be loved prevails, and they stay put.

YOUR CHEATER KEEPS CHEATING
—AND YOU'RE STILL THERE!

♛

Gilda-Gram®
Men feel invaded by too much closeness.
Women feel evaded without enough closeness.

Both genders may strive toward "happily-ever-after" at first, but after some time, many feel cheated—even without feeling cheated *on*. And they're angry. Some women go through torment trying to choose between Mrs. and Mistress status.

A then non-president, Donald Trump, one who knew about cheating on a wife, cautioned all men who think they can get away with cheating. After reading about a 79-year-old grandmother who was convicted of killing her 85-year-old former boyfriend because she was convinced he was cheating on her, Trump blogged, "There's a lesson . . . When you cheat on a woman, even if she's a 79-year-old grandmother in a nursing home, you could be literally taking your life into your own hands. Is it worth it?"

It was the summer of 2006 when the news hit that gorgeous Christie Brinkley's gorgeous fourth husband, Peter Cook, had been bedding down a 19-year-old ordinary girl working in an ordinary toy store. He wined her and dined her, and replaced her toy store job with one in his architectural office.

Brinkley kicked him out the next day, and publicly announced that the amorous architect's new official address would be The Dog House. Their separation was immediate, followed by divorce.

The young girl Peter Cook wooed and bedded concluded that she and the other girls she learned he had trysts with "were all tools of his little game." Now she believed he had been interested only in her for the sex. *Duh! Did she think he pursued her for her worldly intellect?*

It may seem easy to assign titles like "victim" or "homewrecker" to a girl-woman like this. But authors Jenny Offill and Elissa Schappel size up any impressionable girl's state of mind: "Every close friendship offers the same fundamental thrill; someone has singled you out and chosen you, someone who had no obligation to do so." To a young girl, being pursued by a wealthy, attractive man amid the lush landscapes of the Hamptons, especially if the man is married to a sought after mega model like Christie Brinkley, this is a huge ego-booster.

Scientists explain that the prefrontal cortex in young people's brains that deals with decision-making, prioritizing, suppressing impulses, and weighing consequences, won't fully mature until their mid-twenties. So, a young girl-woman naturally operates at a maturational deficit.

YOUR CHEATER KEEPS CHEATING
—AND YOU'RE STILL THERE!

But the concept of young girls having affairs with older married men is not unique. Even the staid Barbara Walters admitted on The View that when she was 19, she, too, had an affair with a man who was married! Mets catcher Paul Lo Duca was scoring off the field with a 19-year-old, too. The girl said that 34-year-old Lo Duca told her he was divorced, but she should have known something was up: they went out only once in public. When he learned news of his divorce was about to hit, he text-messaged her, saying, "I have to speak to you." In Lo Duca's case, another 19-year-old admitted that she, too, had been enjoying sex trysts with him. She also said that he told her he was divorced. How long did this public figure think he could get away with this lie?

Sonia Lo Duca filed for divorce, charging adultery. The fact that she had been a Playboy model made as much difference to her husband as Christie Brinkley's beauty made to Peter Cook. Gorgeousness is no guarantee for keeping a mate faithful. Billy Joel cheated on Brinkley, too. Eric Benet cheated on Halle Berry. Ethan Hawke cheated on Uma Thurman. Kobi Bryant cheated on his stunning wife, Vanessa. Hugh Grant cheated on Elizabeth Hurley. The list of betrayed beauties is long, leaving hurt and anger in the dust.

Billy Crystal jokes, "Women need a reason to have sex. Men just need a place." In truth, men have 2½ times the brain space assigned to sexual drive as women. While rationalizations for cheating are plentiful, aside from the humor or the anger, few people really understand what drives it.

The replacements the men choose for their gorgeous mates don't nearly measure up to the originals. In the New York Daily News, journalist Jane Ridley questioned, "What kind of idiot trades one of the world's most beautiful women for a teenage wanna-be barely out of high school?" Obviously, Peter Cook was the "kind of idiot" who had trouble handling "one of the world's most beautiful women" because he stood in her shadows. Of course, for as long as she was subsidizing his schmoozing and boozing, he was a big shot. But after he was caught, his duplicity in the fast lane didn't draw the same cache.

In all cases of older men with younger women, somebody has to be the grownup—and it stands to reason that it should be the older man. To accept a grownup stance, Cook's superego, the part of the psyche that observes boundaries, had to be as intact as his lover's prefrontal cortex. Obviously, both partiers were dealing a pubescent deck of cards. Growing up can take a lifetime. But it's a vital mission, because your maturity affects all your relationships.

YOUR CHEATER KEEPS CHEATING
—AND YOU'RE STILL THERE!

♛

Gilda-Gram®
We attract not whom we want,
but who we ARE.

So, two babies find each other and play—until their mommies catch them in the sandbox!

If we were to examine who actually does the cheating, it's often the partner who feels overwhelmed by his or her mate's achievements and/or stardom. Peter Cook was ripe to become a cheataholic. Us Magazine quoted the pair's mutual friend, R. Couri Hay, society editor of Hamptons magazine, "Publicly, he accepted his role as a supportive shadow, and understood who the star in the family was. In private, it ate away at his ego and his masculinity."

Deepak Chopra said, "What outcasts most resent, what drives them into paranoia, is being seen as nobodies." This is so true. I believe that in our culture, it is more difficult for men to be in the shadow of their women than it is for women to be in the shadow of their men. And biology may support men's fears of intimidation by their famous female mates. After praying mantises mate, the female consumes the male. And many male insects lose their genitals after sex. So perhaps there is some real evolutionary foreshadowing at the heart of human men's fears.

At one event, onlookers commented that Cook (actually called "a real nobody" by one of his neighbors), "was incredibly deferential" to Brinkley and that "she overshadowed him." To find an innocent and impressionable young thing to boost his diminished ego provided him with necessary nourishment. In the end, he and the young girl boosted each other for as long as they could get away with it.

Following Freudian principles, while a cheataholic's id, or pleasure drive, screams, "Go for it!," an emotionally healthy person's superego, or conscience, will restrain him. Gretchen Wilson's song "When I Think about Cheatin'" describes such a healthy superego:

When I think about cheatin',
I just think about you leavin',
and how my world would fall to pieces,
if I tossed your love away.
Even when I'm tempted by some stranger,
oh, there's never any danger.
I just think about you leavin',
when I think about cheatin'.

A grounded, rather than narcissistic, ego understands that being impulsive and selfish will destroy you and your key relationship. A grownup is someone who makes the effort to consider the realities of the future.

A stable ego controls the impulses of the id,
doesn't box in the superego with ethical constraints,
and balances the reality of each circumstance. Cook
quickly issued a statement saying that he loves his
wife. His statement was similar to the one Lo Duca
released. These guys say they love their wives, but
they are grappling for their own survival, as they
cheat on their women at home with ladies of lesser
status.

Throughout his tryst, Cook appeared in public
always as the protective and solicitous husband.
Apparently, he wanted to maintain "the life" that
accompanied Christie's connections.

♛

Gilda-Gram®
Cheaters satisfy their hunger,
but often get food poisoning.

We have all observed that what goes around,
comes around. New York's former Governor is an
independently wealthy, Harvard-educated lawyer,
the winner of his last election by 75% of the vote,
with a beautiful Harvard-educated lawyer wife who
gave up her own career to cater to his. They had
three teenage daughters in fine private schools, and
every reason to maintain his rich lifestyle and status.
But poisoned by his own power, prestige, and PR, he

narcissistically believed he never actually deserved what he had.

So, disgraced Governor Elliot Spitzer grabbed the very kinds of prostitutes he had prosecuted. In the end, he cheated not only on his elegant and supportive wife, but also on their three innocent children who will undoubtedly require years of therapy and understanding to grasp how their father could disrespect and abandon them as he did. This childhood journey can set a dangerous pattern of distrust for any men who enter their lives.

Chapter 9

A Cheater's Moment Of Passion Hurts Many People

Cheataholism is an affliction of people desperate to swell their ego and reclaim their lost passion. Once they find a replacement partner, their ego gets stroked, and they rationalize themselves as desirable. The source of fulfillment matters less than their personal desperation to recharge what's missing inside.

Unfortunately, as my friend Ellen did, after a cuckolded partner learns of her partner's infidelity, she may question her own self-worth. The biggest problem is that the one betrayed recognized the Relationship Red Flags that were ongoing and evident to others. Before she found out, when asked what the key to her successful marriage was, Brinkley responded, "Honesty."

Ironically, the corporate name for this couple's $60 million estate was Who-Can-You-Trust?" They told the public that was because their belongings are in trust for their kids, but I can't help but wonder whether it was really Brinkley's wishful thinking that her husband would surprise her with fidelity.

It is said that the spouse is always the last one to know. But does a spouse really not know that her mate's beak is growing at the rate of Pinocchio's? It had been rumored that the Brinkley/Cook marriage had been in trouble for some time. Why didn't the two parties recognize this, and do something about it, either through counseling or divorce? Each partner in a marriage instinctively knows when things are not right. But,

♛

Gilda-Gram®
People continue behaviors for as long
as they reap pay-offs.

Many partners prefer not to tango with the truth because it's too painful, and also because it's providing them with material and emotional things they still want. But the longer a transgression continues, the greater the humiliation of the cuckolded party, and the more issues will need to be addressed if the couple does attempt reconciliation.

Of course, when you're rich and famous, there are always rubberneckers to offer their opinions about what went down. Some distinguish between short-term, one-night-stand cheataholism, naming it "meaningless," and long-term relationship philandering, which they deem "devious." *Who constructs these rules of etiquette?* An unnamed family member of Brinkley's adjudicated that it would have been different if Peter Cook had had a "meaningless" one-night stand. *Different for whom?*

This rubbernecking "buttinsky" said that because his philandering was a prolonged and "devious" relationship, it merits greater penalties. In contrast, Sonia Lo Duca's mom said she was told her son-in-law's betrayal was a fling, not a long-term affair, which was the basis of her daughter's filing for adultery. Perhaps she was trying to soften the emotional blow on her daughter by minimizing LoDuca's cheating. For sure, each person who weighs in on this painful situation has a hidden agenda, even if it's to protect his or her friend or relative.

Like the guy at my gym who showed great remorse after his wife finally confronted him about his transgressions that spanned many years, Peter Cook's remorse resulted after the cheataholic had time to think about what he was losing, and how badly he wanted his up-until-then charmed life to return to Camelot.

Melinda had finally decided to divorce her cheataholic husband. It was then that Ed suddenly recognized that he didn't want to lose his wife. During their legal negotiations, she fractured her foot, and was in a more vulnerable frame of mind. So, Ed tried to use Melinda's vulnerability to wend his way back into her heart. While he had never been there for her during any of her medical crises (and she had had a number of them during their 10-year stretch), he suddenly offered to massage her broken foot. Out of nowhere, Melinda said she regained her emotional strength, despite the fact she was physically injured. She sternly told Ed, "It's over; get lost."

Life would certainly be simpler if transgressors considered the consequences BEFORE they got caught in the wrong person's short hairs!

CHAPTER 10

The 7-Year Itch Got Younger

Marriages used to suffer from what was commonly called the "7-Year Itch." The term was such a popular phrase, it became the title of a 1955 comedic movie starring Marilyn Monroe. The storyline depicts a faithful husband whose family goes away for the summer, while he is tempted by a beautiful neighbor. The 7-year mark in a couple's marriage traditionally signaled a shaky relationship time that threatened a union's shelf life.

In a world more time-crunched than it was in the 1950s, it is reported that the number of years it takes for most marriages to derail has slid from seven to four. But more recently and more shocking than the number four are the findings by a study jointly conducted by the University of Wisconsin Center for Demography and Ecology and the Pew Research Center. It found the sizzle has slid even further to three years! Celebrity divorce lawyer and noted marital pessimist, Raoul Felder, names marriage the "first step on the road to divorce."

One researcher found that the 7-Year Itch still exists, if a couple continues to hang on. The Census Bureau says that the average marriage lasts only eight years. So, we can surmise that after the usual two marital dips, at Years 3 or 4, and 7, people finally decide to terminate their relationships during Year 8. It was also found that 43% of unhappy marriages finally break up at Year 15.

Thus, many miserable people may choose to remain miserable for a long eight to 15 years! How do they do that? Many who stay, stray—as their way to tolerate their unhappiness! Unfortunately, the rationalization for a moment's sweetness is often followed by a painful, lengthy payout. Is it worth it? Actually, for some, it may be.

In the movie, "Working Girl," Melanie Griffin's character, Tess, came home one day to find the guy she was living with in bed with one of her friends. Nonchalant about his cheating episode, just three days later, he asked Tess to marry him. Her need to exit her dull life, including him, is what propelled her to reach much higher in her career. She became driven to succeed in business, which she did by impersonating her boss and then romancing her boss' boyfriend.

YOUR CHEATER KEEPS CHEATING
—AND YOU'RE STILL THERE!

Of course, Hollywood is renowned for its sentimental, happily-ever-after endings. Although Tess' boyfriend cheated on Tess, and Boss' boyfriend cheated on Boss, Tess and Boyfriend remained together in love, which culminated in celebrating her promotion. The End.

Real life is usually not so sappy or happy. Very quickly, Tess exorcized her ex from her life and bedded her boss' beau. Few real people have that kind of fortitude and luck to bed-hop without cost.

A study at the School of Public Health at the University of Sydney, Australia, found that Hollywood movies fail to show the negative consequences of rampant sex and drug use. The study cited no depictions of consequences of unprotected sex such as unwanted pregnancies, HIV or other STDs. Only Pretty Woman, in which Julia Roberts plays a prostitute, contained a "suggestion of condom use, the only reference to any form of birth control." Basic Instinct had six sex scenes, no birth control, and no health consequences—although one might deem death by ice pick to be a concern!

More current movies and TV series also avoid discussions of safe sex and protection. I think of Showtime's "The Affair," and all the other bedhopping that occurs without penalty for promiscuity. It's not the real world—and with all the susceptibility that exists, people must be more sexually judicious.

There is an ongoing debate as to whether it is the responsibility of the film industry to set standards that people can emulate. Average people do copy the styles and behaviors of the stars on screen and off. Just look at the influence on our culture the Kardashian family has had! They may have led the way for babies out of wedlock and mixed race couples. For them, if they take a fall, they have a supportive support system to help them up. When the average Jane tries to mirror the job-hopping and bed-hopping, without a huge supportive family, s/he may be faced with deep debt and deep pain. We are NOT "Pretty Woman," we are NOT a reality star, and we do not have endless barrels of cash.

In real life, when someone in a long-term relationship is hurt, s/he may have a fling with a new person out of anger or desperation, or s/he may think such a quick fix will re-build his/her broken confidence. It begins with abundant sex and little commitment. But it's different for the different genders. Dierks Bentley sings it as it truly is:

It's different for girls when their hearts get broke.
They can't tape it back together with a whiskey and
Coke.
They don't take someone home and act like it's
nothing.

YOUR CHEATER KEEPS CHEATING
—AND YOU'RE STILL THERE!

*They can't just switch it off every time they feel
something.
A guy gets drunk with his friends and he might hook
up.
Fast forward through the pain, pushing back when
the tears come on.
But it's different for girls.*

Nothing in life remains the same. Because a fling
has shaky roots, one of the parties may soon vie for
deeper ties. And that's when the other will leave
skid marks faster than she can say, "I'm gone!!"
That's usually when I'll receive an email signed
"What a Fool I Was" from the person willing to
threaten his reliable relationship with a quickie
indiscretion.

Thirty-nine-year-old Peggy was just such a
person. Married for 14 years with two children and a
good job, she complained that she and her husband
had grown apart over the years, and it particularly
showed in their dwindling sex life. When a new
person entered her department at work, she began a
mild flirtation, and then had an affair. She said,
"Although I felt really guilty, I couldn't help being
with him since he made me feel new and alive again.
He professed his love for me and told me that he
would marry me instantly if I were single."

But of course, the new guy cooled his jets after
their sexual encounter got old. He even began to

reiterate her married status as the excuse for his not wanting to continue seeing her. She concluded that perhaps a stale marriage is better than a selfish, flighty player who can't make a commitment. But the real question was whether Peggy was willing to work as hard on her marriage now as she was on the pursuit of temporary emotional stroking.

Peggy had said that she still loved her husband, but that she was no longer *in love* with him. Whenever I hear the "love" vs. "not in love" line, I read that as a signal that the passion they once enjoyed needs a rejuvenating kick in the butt. As long as people do something toward rekindling the fiery embers they once had, there is hope for that relationship's future.

Despite all the odds and all the stories about derailing marriages, in just one week, two middle-aged couples I know, one in Florida and the other in California, chose to suddenly get married. Sure, steady sex has proven to relieve arthritis pain for up to six hours—but none of these friends were in that debilitating a state. Both couples had been living together for a few years, three out of the four people had never been married before, and all had suffered through myriad relationships that did not work. But now, in their 40's and 50's, they were at last bitten by the quest to nest.

YOUR CHEATER KEEPS CHEATING
—AND YOU'RE STILL THERE!

♛
Gilda-Gram®
To be happy and to grow,
be willing to surrender to the unknown.

Chapter 11

So Why Wed?

It wasn't until the 18th century that love became the reason to marry. Today, the wedding industry is huge. There are around 2.5 million weddings every year in the United States. The average wedding budget is $20,000, while the average household income of a newly married couple is only $55,000. So, if the amount spent on weddings every year is a whopping $40 - $70 BILLION, it's clear that many couples go into hock to be able to afford that special day.

Putting so much effort into a one-day event increases the blood pressure of the bride and gloom. With all that stress, it's no wonder we have added the new term, "bridezilla" (and also, not to be upstaged by the future missus, "groomzilla") to our current day parlance.

YOUR CHEATER KEEPS CHEATING
—AND YOU'RE STILL THERE!

The WE network's "Bridezillas" TV show set a series record of viewers. Since then, acting out mates has become the norm on reality TV. Obviously, there is tremendous interest in watching stressful wedding preparations and the craziness that results.

> *New York Observer Bridal Blog: A Tableau Vivant of The Scream, April 28, 2006.*
>
> *I went to MOMA yesterday to take my mind off all the wedding craziness. I wandered into the Edvard Munch exhibit and came across his most famous work, The Scream. I stared at it for a long time, finally recognizing it resembled me and Mitch. Hands on face, mouth wide open and a silent but visible scream bellowing out.*
>
> *It's 25 days until our wedding, and I think we're both starting to freak out. Wedding dead time is long over and we're officially into wedding crunch time. I am five meetings, two fittings, one hair trial, a bachelor and bachelorette party, and a rehearsal dinner away from getting married. I prefer to look at the tasks ahead instead of thinking too much about the wedding day itself. The light at the end of the tunnel is finally visible! –Maureen*

Married couples, whose numbers have been declining for decades, have finally slipped into the minority of American households. Yet, if my own friends are any indication, plenty of people still opt for the promise of wedded bliss. Aiming to avoid any of the usual wedding hoopla, both sets of my middle-aged couple friends simply sent notifications by email *after the deed had been done.*

I emailed back one of the new wives, asking, "What's going on? Two couples I know in their AARP years tied the knot in the same week!" She jokingly attributed it to global warming! Or perhaps, she wondered, if it was the incredible cost of health insurance. She told me that when she announced to an elderly friend of hers that she had gotten married, the woman responded, "Oh, that's so nice. No one's doing that anymore." We laughed, but the truth is that marriage has been around for centuries, and despite the reputed downsides, it continues to beckon couples, young and old, again and again and again.

Research shows that delaying marriage has its benefits. The National Marriage Project at Rutgers University reports that couples can cut the divorce rate in half by waiting to marry after 25 years old, when the brain has had more time to mature enough to decide on such a life-altering decision.

But despite the jokes and bad-mouthing about the institution of marriage, the push toward this union continues. It's just that couples ought to analyze their compatibility a long time before their marriage ends in divorce.

YOUR CHEATER KEEPS CHEATING
—AND YOU'RE STILL THERE!

♛

Gilda-Gram®
A feeling of maximum security lockup
kills two-getherness.

CONCLUSION

Okay, we've seen how marriage has gotten a bad rap. Nonetheless, people keep signing up for it. So, I believe the question is not *whether* to marry. Rather, the challenge people should discuss is *how* to marry. They must understand the pitfalls before they tumble into them. They must recognize that life is not a fairy tale, and there will always be bumps in the road. And they must plan beforehand, so they know how they will respond during times of crisis.

I recommend that no one get married until they have seen their love during chaos. Anyone can put on a happy face when life is going well. But when bad things happen—and they always will, how does your partner cope? Moreover, do you want to be around that person when the sky is falling in?

The things that attract us at first are usually the things that drive us crazy later on. But crazy-making things don't necessarily have to push people into a cheating partnership. Know your mate, really see your mate, invest in your mate, and believe in your mate. Moreover, be emotionally available to your mate, as well.

Life will never go exactly as planned. Margaret Mitchell said, "Life's under no obligation to give us what we expect." But when you're thrown a curve ball, don't make that a signal to run to someone else's bed. Undoubtedly, the problems you had before you ran off, will be the same as those you have when you want to return home.

Find out as much as you can about your potential honey before you commit. If it's already too late, know that 65% of couples that have had a cheating issue decide to remain together. Yes, cheating does not mean that your relationship is kaput.

When a relationship is in trouble, cheating may be a good thing for a pair to be thrown into reality. It could be the necessary kick in the butt two people need to rewire a stale union.

But don't try to walk the path to happiness alone. The 65% of couples that chose to remain together— and that survived—got counseling to determine why the cheating occurred, and how to prevent it in the future. If you need that kind of help, seek it out.

Today, there are therapists like myself who give advice on Skype, on the phone, and through email, from all over the world. Make your objective the desire to stick together for the long haul—and do whatever it takes to manifest that goal. All you need are two people willing to work for the love they once felt.

♦♦♦

For questions so far, contact me at
www.DrGilda.com

Love (of course),
Dr. Gilda

Now onto PART II

Part II: INTRODUCTION

The Traits That Draw You Together Can Also Drive You Apart

A reader commenting to the Editor of Oprah Magazine, said, "While I loved him dearly, in the end, it was his most attractive trait that drove us apart." While this seems peculiar, it's not really. The inconsistencies and ironies of love confound us.

A Country Music song, "Poison and Wine," by The Civil Wars explains:

I wish you'd hold me when I turn my back.
The less I give, the more I get back.
Oh, your hands can heal, your hands can bruise.
I don't have a choice, but I still choose you.
Oh, I don't love you, but I always will . . .

Yes, behaviors that seem wonderful at first because they are exciting and new, can drive us

96

crazy after a while when we realize they are not really so exciting and new anymore.

Sometimes, when you're overwhelmed by difficult traits, you may choose to remain in the relationship for many reasons. The way you cope, however, is to drop out emotionally by quitting your contribution to the union. But dropping out is dropping out, whether you're emotionally present or you choose to physically leave.

♛

Gilda-Gram®
Whether you leave your partner
physically or emotionally,
you're still gone.

CHAPTER 1

The Passion Myth

♕

Gilda-Gram®
Love at first sight is hit and myth.
Lust with potential is real.

When two people first meet and fall ravenously in heat, their hormones fly, based on a mix of brain chemicals that produce irrational behaviors. At this early stage, a couple's main concern is to scratch the hormonal itch that is burning inside. So, with all this combustion at the foot of the rainbow, what happens after two people reach the proverbial pot of gold?

All couples complain that after a while, the passion in their relationship is not what it used to be. A USA Today research report found that when male cicadas sing to attract females, their chorus is louder

in decibels than the sound of city traffic. That's the
kind of first love experiences human partners
remember—and believe should continue forever.
When their dreams dissolve, people become
disappointed and even angry.

The Law of Thermodynamics dictates that all
systems break down or become more chaotic unless
energy continues to be added to them. So, your car
will malfunction unless you maintain it, and your
body will crash unless you sustain it. The same
exists with relationships. Yet, unwittingly, people
often believe that once they cohabitate or tie the
knot, no maintenance is needed again. Try that with
your car or body!

Knowing the mandates regarding our autos and
our physiques, why do we employ a double standard
when it comes to romance? Clearly, relationships
have to be *worked*. That means that people must
expunge the couch potato mindset and deliver the
same kind of emotion they did when they met. Yet,
the tendency for that is unlikely, because people
settle in . . . which eventually translates to just plain
settling.

The promise of passion fools us. It magically
guarantees a lot at first blush, only to let us down
after the flower has bloomed. And that's our fault.
New passion is exciting simply because it is *new*.
It's a surge of emotion that overtakes us. It is
craving, carnal appetite, and walk-into-walls

preoccupation that absorbs us with such intensity, we throb to be close to the object of our affections so that we can do nothing else than objectify! But there are some cautions. Unfortunately, while a one-minute kiss burns six or seven calories, it could intermix 270 colonies of bacteria. That's code for the reminder that all that glitters is not gold.

♛

Gilda-Gram®
**The first touches that lead to caresses,
and the first kisses that lead to canoodles,
have only limited shelf life.**

While passion's lack of longevity may seem disappointing at first, in reality, no one could get anything done if s/he continuously overcome by unrestrained hormones. While most people tend not to judge passion's remission as positive, the truth is that nature actually does us a favor by lifting the burden after a time of mindless yearning.

Beyond that frenzied quivering period, something calmer and more stable takes over. This new state turns out to be more rewarding and enduring than that short period of continued hunger. The new state is called "friendship," but it is usually interpreted by the misinformed majority as "The End."

In her book, Unhooked Generation, Jillian Straus talks skeptically about relationship longevity: "The

one thing that marriage can most reliably deliver—
companionship—just doesn't rate very high on the
desire scale anymore. The prospect today of living a
lifetime with someone who gives you only stability,
a family, and companionship? Grounds for
Valium—or divorce." While this author addresses
the 20- and 30-something demographic, the
downgrading of friendship as a marital asset is
widespread for all ages these days.

Back many years, author and scholar, C.S. Lewis
(1898-1963), said, "Friendship is born at that
moment when one person says to another: "What!
You, too? Thought I was the only one." So, the
harmony of mutual thought always had appeal.
However, Lewis insisted, "Eros will have naked
bodies; Friendship, naked personalities"—thereby
underscoring how passion and friendship are such
separate entities.

For baby boomers, the sizeable population of
people born between 1946 and 1964, a Gallup Poll
reported that only 35% believe that marriage is "very
important" if a couple has a child. Yet, 66% of
respondents of this age agreed that it is "very
important" to get married if a couple plans to spend
their lives together.

But marriage is on the decline. We're still a
marrying society when it comes to demonstrating
commitment to a partner, but not necessarily when it
comes to raising a child! What's that about? This

YOUR CHEATER KEEPS CHEATING
—AND YOU'RE STILL THERE!

American mindset dramatically contrasts European beliefs that marriage is not necessary unless there is a family to raise. Has the disposable relationship concept totally swept the U.S.?

Knowing no better, passion challenged people become alarmed. If they're married, they worry they will fall into the huge portion of the population headed for divorce. If they're single, they rehash their old attempts to keep love fresh—with one flame after another. But whatever their status, the loss of passion causes people to feel like failures, losers at love, and losers at life. Again, knowing no better, they enact the only behaviors they have in their repertoire: they strive to assure themselves that they still have what it takes to be desired, attractive, and in demand.

This is when they seek new partners—because "new" brings back those initial chemical changes that are physically real, even though they can be emotionally misleading. Immediately, their new relationship is one of accommodation, not of convenience, as they had boringly experienced with the person left behind. Little do they know that what they really need to pursue is deep introspection, to decipher what is really happening to them. As much as they may think otherwise,

♛
Gilda-Gram®
An erection does not count as
personal growth or love.

Introspection leads to insight about what the reality is. It is driven by our "Inner Mojo." These internal drivers are based on people's self-esteem, ethics, and personal standards. But many unhappy people mindlessly only want to replace their click-less partner with a substitute. The new somebody serves as their "Outer Mojo," masquerading as arm candy to provide what these seekers lack inside.

They believe that since the passion is gone in their primary relationship, the whole relationship has deteriorated, they're not as attractive as they were at the beginning, and this is the end of the road. For appearances, they might make it seem like the relationship is still strong. They rationalize that they're staying for the sake of "the children," "the money," "the lifestyle," "the dog,"—and I've actually once heard "the goldfish"! But despite what it looks like on the exterior, they really believe their relationship is kaput.

What they are unaware of, however, is that a deep and everlasting friendship can be coupled with the great passion a couple originally enjoyed. They have no idea that their love longevity can expand to greater depths with the addition of friendship. But

103

even if they heard this, would they accept that there could be anything greater than what they once knew as "passion"?

The friendship concept doesn't usually attract a lot of takers. Meanwhile, those who opt to satisfy their momentary needs with another partner only find that the new romance, too, has a limited run— and the cycle of discontent continues . . .

As the now legendary character, Sue Ellen, from the TV series, Dallas, said to one of her rivals: "The mistress always thinks she's smarter than the wife, but if she's so smart, why is she the *mistress*?"

♛

Gilda-Gram®
Marrying your mistress
only creates a job opening
for another mistress.

Circumstances usually don't work out the way many mistresses hope. Some believe that if a married person gets divorced, and re-marries his/her cheataholic lover, that would be the cure for his/her curse. However, a cheater is a cheater is a cheater because the need to continue satiating dwindling desire doesn't end.

So even if the cheater marries, the cheating will begin again once the Passion Deprivation builds. For this reason, it's common to find cheaters cheating on their lovers and their spouses at the same time. Soon enough, that new love object becomes the cozy—and dull—partner the cheater felt the need to betray.

For many people in our culture, the concept of a stable marriage is considered boring. HBO's final season of the Sopranos had Tony falling in love again with his wife after a near death experience. Even when it seems that he's about to stray, and he begins a passionate kiss with a randy realtor who just brokered a deal for him, he is seized with guilt over his faithful wife, and he storms out of the would-be transgression. Not coincidentally, for the first time in Sopranos history, ratings for the show began to plummet!

In contrast, the series that followed the Sopranos, Big Love, depicting a polygamist family, saw its ratings soar, especially as the husband began to cheat behind the backs of his unsuspecting two younger wives—with his third wife, who, incidentally, was his first and oldest wife—*and friend!*

Obviously, cheating dramas draw big crowds. Marital cheating is nothing new. But maybe audiences identify with the waning heat of romance, and they enjoy watching someone else's solution for it.

YOUR CHEATER KEEPS CHEATING
—AND YOU'RE STILL THERE!

Our divorce rate continues, lovers fear abandonment, and people exchange bedmates as frequently as they change their underwear. Yet, if you were to read the emails I receive, it sure seems that people long for love that lasts.

Keeping the temperature to the level it was when two people newly met is unlikely. The reason for that is scientific.

CHAPTER 2

Who We Attract, Why We Attract, And How We Attract

While we would all like to attribute our taste in mates to our own devices, there are many factors that influence who we choose and why, based on scientific data, anthropological realities, and extensive research from varied and different fields. Here are some of the explanations.

WHO *We Attract:*

Who we actually attract into our lives is based on two basic concepts, interspersed with other supporting traits that draw us in: We seek our complementary opposite, and we also attempt to mirror our parents.

For starters, the expression, "opposites attract" is real. We choose mates with traits that are different from, yet complementary to, our own. So, a "morning" person would be intrigued by an "evening" person, a person with a fair complexion would be fascinated by someone with dark and swarthy skin tones, and, as a recent news article exposed, white collar women enjoy blue collar men. Based on this attraction of opposites, we somehow, and misguidedly, believe that two halves are required to make us whole—and the person who has what we believe we're missing will be the perfect mate.

At the same time, also at play is our desire for traits, both good and bad, that we unconsciously recognize from our parents. That's our unconscious ancestral wish list. Unfortunately, the bad traits are more influential in our attraction to a partner. And that's because they give us the opportunity to re-live and heal old wounds inflicted on us during childhood—thereby making us feel that we have grown and overcome our childhood pains.

Cara's attraction to angry men reflected her unconscious desire to work out her childhood issues with her angry father. But she didn't know this when she was feeling depressed after each of her breakups. She needed to learn that anger is depression turned outward.

Once she understood this, she was able to see these men as unhappy creatures that were too miserable themselves to love anyone else. As she explored this in therapy, she recognized that her traits were identical to those of her men. She discovered that, like them, she was unhappy, and looking to fix her past pains with the help of a partner—which can never work.

♕

Gilda-Gram®
We attract not whom we want,
but who we are.

So, both these motives push us to seek a particular person to love: our complementary opposite, and our parents' traits, both good, but mostly bad, with which we learned to be comfortable. Once we unconsciously select a mate based on those two elements, we move to more discriminating refinements.

WHY We Attract:

Our reasons for attraction are predicated on the genes our partner offers that will generate strong and healthy offspring. For example, symmetrical bone structure suggests desirable genetics. Men prefer women's waists to be $60 - 80\%$ the size of their hips to indicate fertility. And women seek men with slightly feminized faces because they reflect individuals who are warmer, kinder, and more trustworthy.

So, generally, men want *honey* from their women, defined as good looks for fertility, and women want *money* from their men, translated into an ability to financially support the offspring.

HOW *We Attract:*

The feeling described as "chemistry" is a scientific process that occurs quickly and sequentially in this order:

1. Dopamine, a brain chemical neurotransmitter, rushes you and pushes you toward the other person.

2. Pheromones, or "smell prints," offer a "come hither" response to your pursuer when they hit that person's hypothalamus in the brain.

3. The hypothalamus directs the body to send out attraction signals. The pupils dilate, the heart pumps harder, the face flushes, there might be some sweating, and the scalp glands release oil for extra shine. (*And you thought it was your conditioner!*)

4. The next day, more dopamine is released as your partner experiences a yearning that propels him to contact you.

5. The brain becomes intoxicated with a cocktail of natural chemicals that produce

irrational, but natural, highs, similar to what occurs when anyone reacts in fear or anger. This unique mix consists of more dopamine, now added to norepinephrine, another neurotransmitter, and phenylethylamine, or PEA.

6. Oxytocin, also known as "relationship glue," bonds the two of you together. Oxytocin is the same chemical that triggers labor contractions, induces lactation, and bonds a mother and her baby. Oxytocin increases during touch—but even the thought of being touched causes oxytocin to flood the body. Both men and women produce it, but women have more of it. Research has suggested that people with higher levels of oxytocin are more monogamous.

That's the general sequence of how partners attract and attach. NBA owner, Mark Cuban, has another take on the attractor factor. While sending someone to pick up girls for him at a New York club, he said, "Just say I'm a billionaire. They'll come over. For every billion dollars I have, my [bleep] gets 10 inches longer." British journalist Julie Burchill concurs: "Wherever there are rich men trying not to feel old, there will be young girls trying not to feel poor."

While seemingly crass, Cuban's conjecture follows the anthropological mindset that men want honey while women want money. I am personally familiar with this theme. My octogenarian grandmother married her third husband because he was the only man she knew who had all his own teeth! To her, this was a blatant sign of prosperity and health.

Author Michele Herman, writing a "Modern Love" column in The New York Times, said that all she had known while driving was how to get lost. So, she married her husband for his sense of direction!! In my book, "Don't Bet on the Prince!," I sorrowfully admit to marrying my husband because I wanted someone who would tend to the annoyances of my car's maintenance!! With the chemical cocktails, the physical preferences, the opposite and complementary attractors, the parental influences, and all these other variables, whom we choose and why is an enormously complex conundrum—and it continues to change.

In the Journal of Marriage and Family, sociologist Julie Press said that women seeking husbands might simply want "cute butts and housework": a physically attractive man who will do dishes. As more women do become "the men they wanted to marry," which was Gloria Steinem's proclamation decades ago, tastes for different traits will continue to change.

Yet, the scientific findings become particularly interesting after that magical three- year threshold of lustful irrationality. Like any drug, over time, the body requires more of this mix of dopamine, norepinephrine, and PEA to achieve the same kind of effect the couple experienced earlier.

In committed and stable relationships, the chemicals give way to a different combination: endorphins, which are other brain chemicals, and oxytocin. This combination calms the mind and kills anxiety, as the drug-like effect creates a healthy interdependence of the pair. This interdependence bonds a couple to exceed the three-year shelf life prediction. In fact, because endorphins and high doses of oxytocin are natural opiates, this period can actually become the most rewarding and enduring time for happy and committed couples.

On the other hand, if the relationship is shaky, and partners don't understand the natural science behind the chemical changes, and the need to take their relationship in another direction, they will personalize their decreased push for passion, and blame it on their own, and/or their partner's, inadequacy. They will misperceive their romantic connection as one that is in trouble. They will seek new partners for the thrill of reclaiming their memory of early love.

CHAPTER 3

The Lure Of Illicit Love

In one of my "Ask Dr. Gilda" columns on Match.com, woman described how she had an affair with a married man for 21 years while they worked together. When the company relocated, that ended the face time this couple enjoyed. In fact, as soon as the office closed, so did this man's heart.

Now the woman said she was living a life of super hell. She was 42 years old, unemployed, and blaming him for having "taken the best part" of her life. She conceded, "I've lied and cheated all these years, and don't know how to make things right." She signed her name, "Depressed with Nothing."

Such is the situation when a "work wife" takes her job too seriously—in the wrong direction. A couple can spend an inordinate amount of time together at the office, and many people consider that their home away from home. If a married person has a willing on-the-job partner who will cavort with him/her in a secret way, the excitement of doing the illicit accelerates the passion—and it's easy to misconstrue this passion as the real thing.

But such feelings are not based in reality, and there are no free rides. Audrey Hepburn had a propensity for bedding down married men. But she didn't like it when the shoe was on the other foot. When she found out that her second husband, a psychiatrist, had been cheating on her, and flagrantly doing so in the bedroom they shared, she said she seriously contemplated suicide. Suicide is no casual threat, as it outranks homicide in the United States, and continues to climb.

What seems like a fun affair may also seem harmless at first. But every act has a consequence, and what goes around comes around—and much more quickly than one would think. I suggested Depressed with Nothing seek a new job at once, at least as a distraction. I then recommended she make a list of the lessons she learned from her secret affair, so she would not repeat them again.

♛

Gilda-Gram®
Adults make choices
every second of our lives.

YOUR CHEATER KEEPS CHEATING
—AND YOU'RE STILL THERE!

As with most affairs, this woman had placed her man on a pedestal, and after he flew the coop she needed to see him as a mere mortal with flaws. Once she saw his warts, she could detonate his throne.

I thought I had responded to this woman's question with dignity and grace, as she was hurting in the worst way. I received hundreds of emails from readers who applauded my comments. But a few people were not thrilled with what I had to say.

One woman furiously accused, "You are unwilling to hold this cheater responsible for the damage her actions caused. In fact, you even want to protect her from any of her self-inflicted repercussions."

And I received an email from someone called "Normal Hot Male" that said, "Anyone with a brain can detect the feminist mindset you present by implying that most men cheat." I asked him to revisit the column and show me where my allegedly "feminist mindset" "intimated" that "most men cheat." Normal Hot Male never wrote back. Typical! But, for sure, nerves are on end over the cheating topic.

There is huge energy around the topic of a single woman cheating with a married man. I don't hear as much resentment when it comes to a single man cheating with a married woman. There are days I wonder why I do what I do. But then, I receive some of the most beautiful thank you notes from those I've touched, and it makes the crazies scatter in the dust.

CHAPTER 4

The Evolutionary Rationale For Cheating

On the heels of Normal Hot Male's accusation against me are Robin Baker's evolutionary principles that hold that the objective of men is to spread their sperm. This is the conclusion of evolutionary biologists who say that monogamy is not natural. In the animal kingdom of 5,000 species of mammals, only 3% take a life-long partner, and even fewer remain faithful to that partner. Most recently, it was found that the ONLY monogamous creature is the freshwater flatworm, which attaches itself to a mate for life.

Men are more prone to cheat than women, according to evolutionary scientists, because:

1. Men can breed more, able to conceive every day if they want, and

2.   We live in a patriarchal culture where men still
     have the abundance of power.

As we've seen with Harvey Weinstein, Bill
Cosby, and too many others, powerful men often
believe they are above the rules. If they are entitled
to a motorcade and other perks, why not also grab
the beautiful woman who is not their spouse?

As men pursue fertility to recklessly spread their
seed, women seek the best genetic input they can
find. That translates into power, success, and
money. Baker contends that 10% of children are not
fathered by the men they call "Dad" (Oh, oh!), less
than 1% of men's sperm is incapable of fertilizing
anything, and a woman is more likely to conceive
through a casual fling than she is through having sex
with her partner (Not a testament for long-term
commitment!)

Since most cultures historically entitle men to
take multiple wives, our culture is unique with our
legal monogamy. While we have these biological
impulses to stray, we are also taught to exercise our
inhibitions against it, and choose to maintain our
sexual and familial reputations above all else. This
is more arduous work for some than it is for others.

Sexual selection is also Darwin's theory. It
promotes that men will compete to sire as many
children as they can, while women opt for fewer
mates while investing in nursing and nurturing their
offspring. Women cherish their kids and men cherish

multiple and beautiful sex partners that are genetically appealing. Emotional skills in men that could engender long-term commitment are absent, while women want their guys to stick around the morning after. If sticking around during just the morning after is such a challenge for men, imagine their resistance to a possible long-term marriage!!

One of the more humorous questions raised about the theory of sexual selection is how it accounts for the persistence of homely males. The Wall Street Journal reports, "If females choose the male with the best traits, as claimed, then after enough generations, every peacock should have a tail to die for. But they do not. Every flock has studs and duds." These opposing scientists hold that many of the traits that females are drawn to have nothing to do with good genes, after all, but rather society's roles. For example, women may lose some of their kinder and gentler aspects as they compete in the "more masculine" work world.

However, despite society's push for change and adaptation, many men still resist substituting the role of sensitive male for hard line macho man. When Normal Hot Man emerges from Sleeping Beauty mode, he can elect to join the debate. I, however, will supplement Darwin's theories with the Why We Attract, Who We Attract, How We Attract Phenomena I described above.

Robin Baker notwithstanding, there is a conception in the midst that it is males, not females, who cheat. In an interview in Harper's Bazaar, Lindsay Lohan said, "I've become like the guy in relationships. Lately I just cannot be in a monogamous relationship." The actress is not alone in her thinking that men cheat, while women don't. Infidelity dates back before the days of the Bible. And anthropologists tell us that it has been on the rise in recent times because of two words: "working women." South Korea's divorce rate is now third in the world, because women are better educated, have better jobs, and feel free to be independent.

Psychologist Shirley Glass found that 50% of unfaithful women and 62% of unfaithful men she treated were cheating with someone from work. Accessibility is a major factor. Whether it starts in the workplace or on the Internet, the ease of developing a secret life elsewhere challenges even the most solid unions. And of course, it's not only men who stray. Many of the unfaithful women are themselves married or committed elsewhere.

Over the course of 54 years, scientists examined the findings of dozens of cases of paternal discrepancy where it was proven that a man was not the biological father of his child. In concert with Baker's findings, although with smaller percentages, it was found that one out of 25 fathers *worldwide* could be raising another man's child without his knowledge.

121

The majority of these "discrepancies" are due to the mother's infidelity during her marriage. How naïve for these mothers to send me emails saying they can't understand why the man they were consorting with suddenly left after they became pregnant with his child. One married woman even complained that only a few months after she discovered her pregnancy, her married boyfriend told her that his wife was pregnant, too. Now she was furious he had stopped calling, with his wife's pregnancy taking precedence.

Anthropology taught us that men are hunters. It's not unusual for a guy to enjoy the chase, but become frightened once the reality of responsibility hits. The chase is fun for hunters. In contrast, many find the actual catch to be quite dull, especially when it's accompanied by a posted sign that reads, "No More Hunting Allowed," which is how many hunters view their marriages. Clearly, a different attitude must prevail:

♛
Gilda-Gram®
Find the "aha's"
amid your "ho-hum's.

Psychology differentiates between the "Madonna" as holy and untouchable mother, and the "Whore" as sexual and available exciter. When a woman plays the role of Whore, life is great for her guy. But as soon as he perceives her as Madonna, he no longer is able to perform his role of Lothario. At first, infidelity talk can be cheap—and rampant. But plans to leave a wife or other plaything usually don't materialize—unless the partner herself discovers the betrayal, and no longer wants to endure the humiliation or the cheating man.

CHAPTER 5

I Still Can't Get No Satisfaction

After the heat of the moment, a new love soon becomes old, and again, the tarnishing of the three-year shelf life creates a desire to look elsewhere to someone with no strings. It's no accident that the antiquated Rolling Stones, who have certainly been around the block a few times, continue to whine, "I Can't Get No Satisfaction." And if these leathery singers in demand by groupies the world over are feeling unfulfilled, imagine what ordinary folks experience.

In a study of 27,500 men and women between the ages of 40 and 80, Edward Laumann, an authority on the sociology of sex, found that there is a gender gap when it comes to enjoying sex. Across the world, men are 10 points more satisfied than women. If the male Stones "can't get no satisfaction," the average

Everywoman must be feeling even more desperately in need for satiation.

Jon Voight, the movie star father of Angelina Jolie, said, "All of us break the rules, the Ten Commandments. Hollywood's excesses hit me, too. When I was young, I got caught up in the celebrity culture. I had an affair. I had a divorce. I lost my head over another woman. If I had it to do all over, I'd have told myself, 'The answer is not in another person.'" But his behavior left scars on his daughter. Today, Angelina has an on-again, off-again relationship with him because he cheated on her mother and left his family for passion in another woman's arms. A friend of Angelina said, "Jon's let her down so many times. She's not willing to give him the chance to let her children down."

Contrast Angelina's approach to her dad with Katherine B. Weissman's story. Her father cheated on her mother, left his children, and moved to Mexico. As chronicled in Oprah Magazine, decades later, she journeyed to find him in that foreign land, to give him love and understanding. Throughout her life, she considered herself a victim who had been abandoned at 14, and heretofore was denied a "secure masculine presence."

When Weissman reached her father at 92 years old and in failing health, she had to fight the 14-year-old's angry memory of being an abandoned teen that still wanted payback for the injuries he inflicted. She said, "Forgiveness isn't an act; it's a process. No, it's a struggle." And then she concluded, "Unless I honor him, I can't have faith in myself."

It has been shown that forgiveness is good for your physical health. Unfortunately, most people learn the lesson of forgiveness too late, after it's already caused emotional damage. Some people never learn the lesson at all.

♛

Gilda-Gram®
If a grudge continues,
the pain remains.

Angelina Jolie would do her health well to understand and accept her father's limitations and admitted foibles. No matter how many new loves a person experiences, or how many babies she conceives and rears, walk-into-walls passion will only last so long—and neophytes continue to fall victim to the temptations that surround them.

When partners seek replacements, how interesting it is that they tend to pursue the same "type" as the one they left behind. Former Friends star, Matt LeBlanc, made tabloid fodder by announcing his split from his wife of three years—and immediately hooking up with his co-star Andrea Anders, who looked much like the wife he was divorcing!

I try to humor people when they tell me they can't go out with this person or that person because s/he isn't their "type." I ask, "Where has your 'type' gotten you so far?" *Duh*!

Okay, okay, apologies to the Rolling Stones, but you still "can't get no satisfaction" with your partner, or you're not meeting your "type" in the singles world, or you are finally admitting that your spouse no longer floats your boat. Have no fear. There are alternatives—or so the techno world advises.

Coming soon will be a multi-sensual experience of virtual sex that will allow you to create a partner of specific dimensions and qualities, who can even whisper sweet nothings in your ear while the two of you are interacting. This new field is called "Teledildonics," and it already allows people at two remote computers to manipulate electronic devices such as vibrators from afar.

Steve Rhodes, president of Simulate Entertainment says he has sold thousands of these Internet-connected sex toys already. But during a radio show where I discussed these new appliances, I cautioned people that no matter how advanced techno-sex becomes, we still need human contact to feel fulfilled.

In the 1950s and '60s, Harry Harlow experimented with infant monkeys to try to determine their reactions to surrogate "mothers" in the form of either heavy wire or wood covered with soft terry cloth. He found that although the wire "mother" provided milk from a nipple, the infant preferred the cuddly cloth surrogate. Harlow concluded that even comfort food does not trump the necessity for touch.

Later, other researchers found that the lack of maternal touching and rocking of an infant results in incomplete or damaged development in the part of the brain that controls "trust," "affection," and "intimacy." These traits eventually form our capacity for "pleasure," "bonding," and "love." So even though Halle Berry's flick, "Perfect Stranger," shows her pleasuring herself as the off-camera voice of Bruce Willis dictates instructions over a computer, the need for human touch in the flesh continues to outweigh all other attractions.

So, newfound sex robots, as mechanically efficient as you may be, you'll never deliver the emotional intimacy that humans need for survival!

CHAPTER 6

Sexual Reaching

Our supply of affection and bonding in this culture certainly seems bankrupt. However, don't be too quick to give up on our appetite for them!

Customarily, the porn industry's mandate is to pack as much fornication as possible into a short period of time. But a new production, "Angela 3," broke a new taboo in porn by showing two people actually engaged in *emotional intimacy*! Never before seen in this genre, fans and critics loved it, and it soared as one of the best-selling films of 2017. It also won six Adult Video News Awards, equivalent to the Oscars of porn! Yes, emotional intimacy in porn is an oddity that has not been seen before—but now that it has, there will undoubtedly be more of it.

People continue to seek out new partners, and are forever sexually reaching, as though that's the answer to the emperor's new woes. But porn's technical explorations are now proving to be trumped by the emotional intimacy that a thirsting society really wants.

Too many people are willing to trade in partners with limited warrantees. But if we are ever to find that elusive thing called "satisfaction," we must construct a healthy environment where deep affection can support it. And that environment does not come gift-wrapped under the guise of sex.

Harlow's experiments showed us the importance of human contact. Questing for sustenance from bonding, people may have sex with someone they have no feelings for, just so they can be held. Such a coming together may involve sex, but it certainly isn't motivated by it. During a Dating & Relating Chat I hosted on MSN.com, I was asked, "Is being with someone just to avoid loneliness ever justified?" That reminded me of the line in the movie, "Jerry Maguire," where the protagonist tells his new love, "You complete me." Sorry, everyone. As inviting a thought as that might seem, nobody can complete anybody.

♛

Gilda-Gram®
We must be complete on our own.

DR. GILDA CARLE

Only out of strength can a solid partnership evolve. But if you're desperate, you'll attract just another desperado. And that's what made you a lonely, desperate seeker in the first place.

CHAPTER 7

Rubbernecking Into Other People's Lives

A New York Times article titled "(Name Here) Is a Liar and a Cheat" reported that Online Dater Magazine estimated 30% of personal ads online are from married cheaters. Singles looking for love online say that they often encounter lots of these losers. A cottage industry has obviously taken the Internet by storm. Sites like DontDateHimGirl.com, WomanSavers.com, and TrueDater.com were formed to protect the innocent and unsuspecting by unearthing the names of liars, cheataholics, thieves, and psychotics before they break any more hearts.

With these sites, the slogan, "You Got Mail" was upgraded to "You Got Nailed!" There is also high-tech spyware that allows skeptical spouses to become armchair sleuths. The need and interest in having such watchdog services is evident as some of these sites receive up to 300,000 hits per day.

Cheating stories attract huge attention in the media. Here are some typical blind items from the infamous Page Six in The New York Post:

WHAT morning TV host is now living apart from his wife because she hired a private eye who bugged his car? The hidden microphone caught him having an affair with a lovely young reporter.

WHICH Democratic party moneybags is getting divorced because he diddled with a candidate's daughter? To cap it off, his wife, the mother of his children, then had a go with her personal trainer (a woman).

WHICH handsome nightlife impresario not only cheats on his gorgeous wife, he also cheats on the gorgeous model who works the door at his newest club in Las Vegas? "The wife is too embarrassed to leave him after all they've been through," said our spy, "so she deals with it."

If these items are true, some spouses have some major explaining to do. But frankly, if the gossip columns already have the dirt on these folks, their mates are probably not far behind.

--What Would You Do If You Were Kevin Costner's Wife?

YOUR CHEATER KEEPS CHEATING
—AND YOU'RE STILL THERE!

Kevin Costner allegedly masturbated while getting a massage at a prestigious hotel in Scotland. He was accused of removing his towel, exposing himself, and then performing the sex act. Costner's wife, Christine Baumgartner, was furious, and allegedly moved out.

--What Would You Do If You Were Connie Chung?

A $100 million lawsuit for sexual harassment filed against Maury Povich by an employee also included tawdry details of the talk show host's "long time, intimate and sexual relationship" with his 47-year-old producer, describing the show set as rife with porn and booze. The accusations threatened to tarnish the image of Povich and Chung, who wed in 1984 and have a son. Chung declined comment.

--What Would You Do If You Were Khloe Kardashian?

Khloe gave birth to a daughter, just days after news broke that Tristan Thompson, the Cleveland Cavaliers star was unfaithful to her with multiple women. But Khloe remained by his side—and even wants to marry him and have more of his babies. She's not even asking him to sign a prenup, because she wants to let him know she trusts him.

--What Would You Do If You Were Staci Felker?

Traveling Troubadours frontman, Evan Felker ghosted his wife, Staci, as soon as he hooked up with Miranda Lambert. She detailed that she perfected homemade chicken soup for when he was sick, and she cared for him when he was coming off benders. She was sent to the hospital and couldn't reach him. She angrily said, "That's not a real man. That's not a country boy and certainly no cowboy. Not a husband I'll ever take back because I was scared and he was gone. Again."

You can see the different ways people deal with infidelity. How would you??

♛
Gilda-Gram®
There is life after infidelity.
But it takes work.

Your willingness and ability to determine the emotion behind your path reflects your power! Some betrayed partners prefer to live in denial, and that's how they go on. Similar to the word "honesty" mentioned by Christie Brinkley during an interview that questioned her secret to marital longevity, Connie Chung said "telling the truth" was the secret to her marriage to Povich.

Obviously, Chung's interview was taped prior to the filing of the lawsuit against her husband and the show. Because there are no free rides, eventually, everything we deny catches up with us!

The interesting part of all this is how fascinated we onlookers are with the rich and famous that cheat! The ratings on an MSNBC TV show that Chung and Povich were doing skyrocketed after the news. However, the public is fickle, and this sort of fascination is short-lived. The show was cancelled after six months of disappointing ratings, except for that one week after the lawsuit came to light!

CHAPTER 8

The Fear Of Lovelessness

♛

Gilda-Gram®
You will never be loved
if you can't risk being disliked.

Emperor penguins have sex only once a year for a period of two to three minutes. Without realizing it, humans fear they will morph into the same situation if they don't remain hot. Often, when a couple splits, even if the ink isn't yet dry on their separation agreement, many rush out with new suitors. There is so much fear about feeling alone and abandoned, many newly single people jump to the next most convenient partner to dull what they sense is the pain from being solo.

By not taking the necessary time to discover:

a.   what went wrong in your last relationship?

b.   how did you contribute to the train wreck (even if it was just by being there)?

c.   how do you intend to heal to avoid heartache the next time around?

Typical of the fear most people feel after a divorce, beautiful Uma Thurman said she was scared she might never find love again. She noted that because of her celebrity status, the accompanying "media circus" would be off-putting for any normal guy. Undoubtedly, that fear contributed to her immediate jump from her long marriage into the arms of Andre Balazs for two years—and why that new relationship didn't work. It couldn't; she had not had enough time to grieve the end of her marriage.

But she returned to Balazs after spending time alone. You need to breathe new space after a divorce, to learn who you were during your marriage, and what you need to change for the future.

Reactionary Rebounding happens so quickly, any love that may evolve from the union doesn't stand a chance. For example, take the friendship between Heather Locklear and Denise Richards. At one time, they were BFFs. Then Locklear was divorcing Bon Jovi rocker, Richie Sambora, and Denise Richards was divorcing Charlie Sheen. Suddenly,

Richards and Sambora became an item, and Locklear was less than pleased by the news.

To onlookers, it would seem that a Hollywood Minute lasts even shorter than a minute in New York! Meanwhile, neither couple was divorced yet. But the Love Triangle quickly became a Love Rectangle when comedian David Spade hooked up with Locklear. (At least, she was not alone anymore.) The bullets really began to fly when Spade publicly accused Richards of being a backstabber, saying that his new girlfriend was, "still nursing the knife wound in her back."

But true to form, the Spade/Locklear duo lasted only six months, and later they declared that they were the typical "just friends." Years ago, when I had interviewed Heather Locklear for the now-defunct Mademoiselle Magazine, she impressed me as a woman with her two feet on the ground. After her initial hurt over her marital breakup, she undoubtedly recognized that Reactionary Rebounding can be a temporary fix.

From these accounts, and others regarding rich and famous couples, it seems that there are only a few people to date in Hollywood. Moreover, these few all play a slick parlor game called "Interchangeable Beds."

While one is left to wonder who is cheating with whom in the civilian world devoid of the Hollywood headlights, the public is vociferous against cheating with the ex of an ex best friend. Selling T-shirts with the logo Team Heather and Team Denise on them, popular LA clothing store, Kitson, had the Heather T's selling at 87%, while the Denise T's were selling much less, at 13%.

An In Touch Magazine poll asked whether Heather should forgive Denise. A whopping 94% said "No." Even the New York Times weighed in on this dilemma, with an article titled, "Coveting Thy Neighbor's Ex." Most people interviewed agreed that dating a friend's ex is a cardinal sin, violating that special code of female sisterhood. Women, especially, place strong value on their friendships, and to betray a girlfriend with whom they've shared so much can cause great pain.

How much of this history contributed to Heather Locklear's journey in and out of rehab is a question we'll never be able to answer. And it raises the old chicken vs. the egg controversy. But it surely proves that beauty, fame, and fortune mean little compared to our health and peace of mind.

Rosemary was seeing Bob for six years. It was a very rocky romance from the start. During their time together, she discovered him cheating on her--and often. They fought, they broke up, but they always went back together. Through all the sick and sin, one of the things that kept them intact was their group of friends that resembled a family. They had all gone to school together, and after they graduated, they kept in close contact. Among the group was Al, who Rosemary always considered to be a nice guy.

Suddenly, Rosemary's father was diagnosed with a terminal illness. At once, she decided to make some major changes in her life. She broke up with Bob, much to his dismay. A few weeks later, her friends attended her dad's funeral. After the event, Al and she walked along the water as she cried. The pair explored the meaning of life and where their futures were going. His consoling words brought her comfort. As a good friend, he continued his support throughout the next several weeks. Then one day, while they were having lunch, he kissed her. He said that he could no longer contain the feelings he had for her. She was realizing that she felt the same for him, as well. But it was only three weeks after she had disengaged from Bob, who was also a friend of Al's. How would they handle the predicament?

Al told Bob the truth, and Bob accepted it, understanding that he and Rosemary would never live happily ever after. Today, Al and Rosemary have been married for three years, and they just had an adorable baby boy. Bob was able to come to terms with bygones without holding grudges. Al and Bob continue to be good friends. So, despite what the polls and the public say, not every story of dating the ex of an ex best friend is the same as the Locklear/Richards debacle.

YOUR CHEATER KEEPS CHEATING
—AND YOU'RE STILL THERE!

However, as much as I research this issue, it seems that some people follow their own rules when it comes to who's dateable and how soon. While Britney Spears and Justin Timberlake were an item, Timberlake's best friend, choreographer Wade Robson, cheated with Britney. This trend of mate poaching seems to be on the rise—and many people, devoid of ethics or conscience, steal a mate from a friend or acquaintance, either for a one-night stand or more.

Timberlake returned Britney's favor by breaking up with her and Wade—and writing a song about it. Later, Justin said, "I dated Britney half my life, but I don't know that person anymore. I'm not sure I knew her before." Too many people are half asleep and emotionally barren while in relationships that profess love.

Even if a person is forgiving, there is still a downside to running off with a friend's mate or ex. In college, my then boyfriend and I double-dated often with Muriel Something and her fiancé. Our two couples broke up within months of each other. Muriel's fiancé asked me out, but I refused because it felt too incestuous to date him. But when my ex-boyfriend asked Muriel out, she accepted without a thought about hurting my feelings.

After I discovered the news, I confronted my ex about his quick-moving, tacky behavior. His excuse? "We were only talking about you." *I told him to go—and he didn't even take the time to thank me for the directions!*

Feelings aside, we must be fair here. Once someone ends a relationship, whomever they rebound with afterwards and how soon the new bonding occurs, is really nobody's business. A former relationship is over, so there are no longer any strings or rules. What only remains is ethics and human decency.

On Planet Earth, emotional ties take a while to come undone. When people discover that their ex is immersed in another love *the moment* they split, they do feel emotionally battered. It's bad enough that they officially ended their love, but to see their former partner with someone new so quickly questions the significance of what they had shared.

Perhaps even more painful is to see a former partner with someone they considered a "friend." That questions not only the significance of the past relationship, but also the meaning of the friendship they believed they had. In my case, I never spoke to Muriel Something again. Today, so many years and relationships later, the seeming slight by that girlfriend and that ex has absolutely no meaning to me whatsoever. Again, the opposite of love is not hate; it's indifference.

CHAPTER 9

How Some People Stave Off Loneliness

Loneliness is more about *feeling* alone than about *being* alone. It's a lonely person's belief, whether real or imagined, that s/he doesn't matter to anyone. While singles comprise 27 million households and rising, even married partners can feel lonely when communication and understanding break down. Lonely people want desperately to connect, but their fear of rejection prompts them to stay away, which in turn, creates more isolation. Reba McEntire's song, "Once You've Learned to be Lonely," sums it up accurately:

Once you've learned to be lonely,
And lonely is the only thing you've known,
It begins to feel like home.
It becomes your comfort zone.

In other words, loneliness can be habitual. Oprah Magazine says this chronic emotional ailment affects up to 15% of the population. And as it becomes more habitual, it wreaks havoc on a person's vitality and self-esteem.

The best way to ward off these feelings is through human contact. How convenient that a new industry has sprung up for "emotional service dogs" that are allowed to accompany their owners into restaurants, offices, health spas, and onto airplanes. Some folks carry around a doctor's note to prove their pet's necessary support to their psychological or emotional well being.

A 2003 Department of Transportation ruling for planes stipulates that animals used to aid people with emotional ailments, like depression or anxiety, be given the same access and privileges as animals helping people with physical disabilities, like blindness or deafness. So, believe it or not, airlines now grapple with how to accommodate 200-pound dogs, monkeys, miniature horses, cats, and even emotional-support goats and ducks, one of which had been dressed up in people clothes! Observe the lengths to which people will go to ward off feelings of aloneness or to dispel the shame of abandonment. Also observe what people will do to insure feelings of approval continue.

To overcome the threat of being solo and scared, some singles pack backup lovers called "sandbags."

YOUR CHEATER KEEPS CHEATING
—AND YOU'RE STILL THERE!

They carry on with their backups behind the backs of their committed partnerships. These jiffy-lovers are already in place when the inevitable jilting of the sure-to-be-dumped occurs. Instead of investing in information gathering as to why their relationships began and ended as they did, they look to deaden the pain in the form of human bandages. But the plan never works as hoped.

> _New York Daily News_, _"Boys on the Back Burner," By Jo Piazza, May 4th, 2006 –The same way physical sandbags are used to shore up a levee in case of a major breakdown, preventing flooding and catastrophe, the metaphorical sandbag is a future lover you have waiting in the wings to dull the pain of a bad breakup._
>
> _"When you end a relationship, it is easy to be sad and mopey, but if you have a sandbag, you fall right into something fun and exciting," Manhattanite Eliza, 25, tells us (all subjects asked their first names only be used). "It's new yet also familiar, since you've been keeping it on the back burner for a while."_
>
> _You may not actively court them or even fantasize about them. You might just keep in touch with a quick, flirty email, text message or voice mail once every six months, just to make sure they still have a fleeting interest in you._

*"People are so terrified of being without anyone that they are willing to create a chorus line," says relationship expert **Dr. Gilda Carle**. "One of my clients had a boyfriend, but actually had a man on the side who she called not by his name, but by his function, Plan B!"*

Sandbagging is the new Hollywood special. Denise Richards' relationship with Richie Sambora didn't happen overnight, nor did Heather Locklear's rumored whirlwind fling with David Spade. You can bet these guys were lined up well in advance of the big split.

"I had a 'sandbag' for five years that I kept around just in case," says Randi, 30. "I gave up my baby blanket in three years, so you can only imagine my attachment. I kept him around with false promises, etc., and saw him once a month to make sure he wouldn't go anywhere."

Then she ran into him - while with a current boyfriend. That's when the sandbag really came in handy. "I turned bright red. My boyfriend broke up with me and even though I never actually dated the sandbag officially, I kept him around and he cushioned the fall."

For most, sandbagging is another option in the back of your mind, for picking up the pieces in case a current romance fails.

YOUR CHEATER KEEPS CHEATING
—AND YOU'RE STILL THERE!

But overlapping an actual relationship - and your backup - is just jerky. "I've gone outside to 'have a cigarette' after sex with my girlfriend, but really just to call back-burner girl," Tom, 27, admits.

He blames his two-timing on relationship "ADD." "Luckily, my girlfriend never found out."

"Sandbag," "Backup," or "Back-Burner" – whatever you name your next-in-line, when that person finds out s/he was only a filler, watch out for the avalanche that follows. The client I describe in the newspaper piece above broke up with Plan A, became tired of Plan B, and ended up totally alone, needing to work on her self-esteem issues, after all. That's when she began therapy with me. I don't know whether it's worse to have a Back-up or to be a Back-up. But no matter at which end of the stick you find yourself, to get over the pain once and for all, there's no escaping the need for heavy duty introspection. Otherwise, you'll repeat your same problems with just another body.

Katie was a newly divorced woman of 45, trying to start over and find a new life. She met Tim when he was allegedly unattached. But a month after dating, he informed her that they wouldn't be seeing each other anymore because his ex-girlfriend had resurfaced, and they had reconciled. When they met, he had neglected to tell Katie he had spent two years with this other "former girlfriend."

After a month apart, he phoned Katie and begged to see her. She agreed to meet him. He told her how much he missed her, and that even though he was now with his ex, he was not in love with her.

Katie and Tim began to see each other behind his girlfriend's back. He told her he could never give her the commitment she wanted, because he could never give that to anyone, despite his deep feelings for her. She cherished the exciting and fulfilling sexual relationship they shared.

He told Katie to date other people, since he had his girlfriend. But every time she went out with someone, Tim would become jealous and say he knew she'd be leaving him soon.

Like most superb rationalizers in lust, Katie fancied herself an insightful reader of hidden agendas. She insisted that Tim really did have feelings for her, but he was just emotionally afraid of those feelings, so he withheld them. Yet, she admitted that she saw nothing but pain coming from this affair. She said that her friends repeatedly told her to leave Tim, but she defended her stance by repeating that her friends didn't see the man that he really was: good, warm, caring, and loving. Yet, she told me, "I've cried many tears, thinking that on nights he doesn't call me, he's with her." She set up an appointment with me to decide what to do next.

I asked how Katie could describe this guy as "good, warm, caring, and loving"—especially while he was cheating on his girlfriend with her! While she might have been legally divorced, she was much too emotionally desperate to be involved with anyone so soon after the end of her marriage. As a result, Tim was getting his cake and eating it, too. And the only reason he was able to get away with such rich dessert was because Katie was spoon-feeding it to him.

I asked Katie what she loved about this loser. Was it his abundant honesty? Katie was a Reactionary Rebounder because she was scared to be alone, and she was afraid to take the time to find an emotionally available man. All Katie did was cry. Tears alert us that we must purge the stress that is overwhelming us, in the same way that sweat removes salt, urine rids waste, and expelled mucus discharges trapped bacteria. So, I told Katie that her tears were her signal that she must make a change NOW. She understood my point, but she didn't know how to distinguish among hanging out alone, carefree flirting, and out-and-out dating. I assured her that if she stayed with Tim, she would be that much more in the dark for never having experienced their differences.

♛

Gilda-Gram®
You are your most perfect lover.

CHAPTER 10

The Line Between Flirting And Cheating

People always ask me whether lingering looks, smiling, and intense eye contact between two otherwise engaged people comprise flirting or cheating. The way I see male/female interaction is that there are gradations of flirting. If your guy smiles sweetly at a pretty waitress, he's letting her know he finds her attractive. After all, cut the guy some slack; he's not dead! But if he begins to touch her, if he asks for her phone number or email address, or if he's staring so hard that he's committing ocular intrusion, that's flirting gone too far—AND it's disrespectful cheating.

The reason this is such a hot topic is because there is no clear definition in our vocabulary of what cheating is and what cheating is not. Of course, that fiasco with Bill Clinton didn't help matters. But

even if there were a rulebook on what constitutes
cheataholism, what one person's tolerance for
straying is might be unacceptable to another. Each
situation is different, and each person has a different
threshold. Within that confusing context, I
differentiate flirting from cheating in this way:
There is a difference between flirting (with a lower
case "f") and Flirting (with an upper case "F").
Lower case "flirting" is the harmless encounter with
that pretty waitress. But upper case "Flirting" entails
anything beyond that, which suggests there's more to
come.

The former Prime Minister Berlusconi of Italy, a
married man, said to one woman, "I'd go anywhere
with you," and to another he said, "If I weren't
married, I'd marry you." Veronica Lario, his wife,
wrote a front-page newspaper letter that said, "To
my husband and to the public man, I therefore ask
for a public apology, not having received one
privately." He did apologize, in another newspaper.
Would you accept the apology? Would you forgive
your mate for such a public indiscretion?

Even with the distinction between "flirts" in
lower case "f" and "Flirts" with a capital, the
behavior of some transgressors is not so obvious.
When Joanne met Lincoln, she thought he was
terrific. He was great to look at, he had a wild sense
of humor, he was Vice President for a large diamond
business, he had a condo in New York City and a
summer home in New York's posh Southampton, he

was active in his church, and he was very, very, very social. This would be a particular great catch for her, because she had been working around the clock, and she knew that she needed prodding to develop her social presence in her town. When Lincoln put the moves on her, he fit the bill for what she thought her future should be.

The couple dated in a monogamous relationship for six months, and all seemed to be going well. They weren't living together, but they saw each other every weekend, and a few times during the week. Then Joanne needed some minor surgery, which put her out of commission for 10 days. Since she was now plugged in to Lincoln's social network, her new friends called her often to check up on her and to chat. One of them casually revealed that while Joanne was recuperating, Lincoln was spotted having dinner with his former girlfriend.

That news didn't exactly speed up Joanne's recovery. When she confronted Lincoln, he did not deny having dinner with his ex, but he dismissed it as his ex needing some friendly advice about a boyfriend she was seeing. Joanne quietly wondered why he had not just come out and told her, rather than choosing to sneak around, knowing that he could possibly be caught in this gossipy town. Rather than let bad feelings linger, she dismissed the incident altogether.

On another occasion, after spending a glorious weekend with Lincoln on the sands and ocean by his house, she chose to return to the city early to get ready for work on Monday. He said he'd watch the tennis match on TV, then leave for the city later. They agreed to speak the following day. On Tuesday of that week, one of the women Joanne had become friendly with asked why she hadn't joined Lincoln at the big party on Sunday night. Joanne hadn't even known about it. Now upset, she dialed Lincoln's digits and asked why he hadn't invited her to go with him to the party. This time, he dismissed his behavior by casually saying he hadn't known whether he was even going, but then, on his way home, he decided to just stop by. Again, Joanne wondered why he hadn't mentioned the party all weekend. *Hmm!*

On still another occasion, while the couple was enjoying a quiet dinner at a local restaurant, Lincoln became overly friendly with the sweet, young waitress serving them. He inappropriately put his arm around her waist while ordering! Joanne told him she felt disrespected and angry. As usual, Lincoln casually dismissed his actions as just having fun and making a stranger feel good about herself.

The number of incidents where Lincoln's behavior was suspicious kept growing. One of the men in the Hamptons asked Joanne out, and when she told him that she had an exclusive relationship with Lincoln, he said, "Oh, I thought the two of you

155

had broken up." At once, she realized that this also-very-social guy had seen Lincoln out with his many lady "friends" at social events to which he was constantly invited as their escort. Early in their romance, Lincoln had informed Joanne that he wanted to continue his platonic friendships with these females he knew, because it was great for his business. How could Joanne fault Lincoln's business ambitions?

But now that Joanne realized these "friends" were considered "dates" by everyone in their circle, she became resentful. She hated Lincoln's slippery, sneaky behavior, his secretive ways, and his avoidance of all discussion regarding her feelings. She began to perceive this love of her life as a lot of sizzle, and no steak! He was a pretty boy, with substance that was a mile wide, but only an inch deep. And apparently, he was a jilting gigolo, as well. Yet, it was summer time and Joanne enjoyed The Life in the Hamptons she wanted to, at least, maintain until the end of the season. So, she swallowed her pride and let things ride—while secretly crying herself to sleep each night.

Then one evening, while they were at a party together, Joanne missed a step on the host's patio and twisted her ankle. Lincoln was busy sweet-talking and laughing with some ladies nearby. She summoned him to get her some ice. He dutifully returned with chucks of ice wrapped in a paper napkin, which immediately tore apart. He clumsily put the remaining ice cubes in her hand and directed her to hold them against her swollen wound. Then he vanished to continue his frivolity, leaving her alone in her pain.

Joanne finally saw the light, and this time, it was so bright, it nearly blinded her. She flashed on the image of him driving a red Mercedes on loan from an ex-girlfriend when his own car was in the shop. She flashed on his expensive leather bomber jacket that was a gift from another ex-girlfriend. She wondered if he "put out" in exchange for all this booty. Oh, Lincoln was a practiced lothario—with all the platitudes and vapors!

When the pair returned to his car together one evening, in her rage, she called him a male prostitute. (It could be argued that she, too, had prostituted herself by deciding to stay with Lothario until the end of the summer season, despite her unhappiness.)

After she became calmer, she simply and soberly told him it was over. He looked like a scared rat, desperately trying to talk her out of her "misconstrued" perceptions. He firmly underscored that during the two years they were together, he had never *slept with* any other woman. *Sure, he didn't have to.* He was a cheataholic who got off on the ecstasy of the admiration by multitudes of women. Putting Flap A into Slot B would have been superfluous. He had already gotten his ego jolt! She said, "Good riddance," and at last she was free.

♛
Gilda-Gram®
Say "I count"
before you say "I care."

Lincoln Flirted with a Capital "F." His disrespect for Joanne and their relationship clearly defined him as a cheataholic. If he were here now, he would argue against this, since his definition of cheating, even before the days of Bill Clinton's revisionist vocabulary, was sexual intercourse. But Joanne decided that no self-respecting woman would buy his excuses. Sadly, it took her a long while after her divorce to build her self-respect. But once she had it, it was hers for life.

CHAPTER 11

Emotional Cheating

Emotional cheating consists of the affair you don't want to admit you're really having. In this age of high tech, adultery au currant suffers from yet another twist. Two people—married to others—enjoy long phone calls, emails, texts, social media interactions, and deeply personal heart-to-hearts. Soon the conversations move from non-important things to their dissatisfactions with their partners. They develop silent crushes on each other, they flirtatiously confide in each other, and especially if they are working together, they depend on their intense connection to get them through each day.

Their new "soulmate" pumps up their feelings of attractiveness and intelligence more than anyone else. But they rationalize the old "Flat A into Slot B" mantra, that "nothing happened," which conveniently translates into, "We never had intercourse," so it's not "sex," and naturally, it's not cheating.

They will tell others that this new friendship is "no big deal." However, this arrangement is secret and deceptive from their partner at home. It is a betrayal of the person waiting in the wings because it breaches the aspect of trust on which every healthy relationship must be based.

Thom was a professional painter whose clients lived in very wealthy communities. He was constantly in people's businesses and homes, interacting mostly with women. He had been married to Marge for 30 years, and they had a solid relationship. Since they had no children, they worked together to build a very successful business. Marge stayed home and scheduled Thom's bookings, and she also sent out the invoices, kept his equipment clean, ordered new supplies when needed, ironed his shirts and jeans, prepared his meals, and generally provided backup so he could do the fine work he was reputed to do, and look clean, well-groomed, and well-nourished when he arrived at each job. Thom was considered to be a "nice guy" by everyone he worked for. And he was so successful, Marge had to schedule his work months in advance.

But now in his early 50s, not unlike many men with more life behind them than ahead, he was

beginning to question where his life was going. All
he did was work, except for Sundays, when he would
stay home, work around his own huge compound, or
meet friends on his boat. He and Marge spent every
Saturday night on a date of some kind. Often, they
met with guys Thom knew since high school, along
with their wives. Out of everyone they knew, Thom
admitted that he was the only one who had never
cheated on his wife. But he sure thought about it a
lot. And now it was beginning to consume him.

All Thom's friends bragged about the women
they had on the side. Thom had watched his friends'
wives get "fat and sloppy," as he described them.
Marge had put on a lot of weight, and Thom said he
could not stand women who "let themselves go." He
described his sex life as dull after all the years he and
Marge had spent together. He wondered what else
was out there.

Occasionally, Thom would meet his friends late
Friday night at a local pub. He said he enjoyed
dancing with the women whom he had known for
years. "They all know I'm married," he announced,
so it was "no big deal" that they were dirty dancing
with him. Without considering them for what they
were, he was already having these mini emotional
affairs. But he insisted that he knew, and they knew,
nothing would come of any of this. He also said that
Marge knew where he was and with whom.

YOUR CHEATER KEEPS CHEATING
—AND YOU'RE STILL THERE!

I cautioned Thom that this alleged "innocence" is the way many affairs begin. I have not met a lot of people who consciously seek out an affair-mate. Yet, I warned Thom that a couple of elements were in place that could prove dangerous to his marriage:

1. He was now questioning his state of life in his 50s.

2. His male friends cheated and bragged about it, making him feel he was missing out.

3. He rationalized that Marge knew where he was and with whom, so his hanging out with his cheating buddies was "no big deal."

4. All the women with whom he dirty-danced knew that he was married, and many of them actually knew Marge.

Because he and Marge were suffering from Passion Deprivation, Thom was ripe for the plucking. After all, he was a wealthy, good-looking guy who women were forever hitting on. How long would it be before he swallowed the bait?

I pointed out that no woman he met would be able to replace Marge. "These chicks who want a quick roll in the hay won't do your billing, clean your clothes and equipment, and be emotionally supportive of you in your old age." I cautioned, "If

Marge finds out you've strayed, don't think she'll give you a moment's peace ever again. Would you prefer to sleep at night, or do you want to fear a Lorena Bobbitt seeking retribution?" Thom considered the options, but he insisted that he just had a lively imagination of what he might do—if he were single. I suggested he fantasize to the hilt, but be careful about acting on these fantasies.

♛
Gilda-Gram®
Fantasize, but answer this:
"Could I replace the person I have at home?

CHAPTER 12

We're Just Friends . . . And Other Lies They Tell You

In our "Don't Blame Me" culture, it seems that everyone's got an excuse for behavior they commit that's not up to par. They blame the person who promised to leave his/her spouse and never did. They blame that person for not recognizing how valuable their relationship was. They blame the person's spouse for being abrasive or inconsiderate or disinterested—as though they knew the truth. They blame the cheater's conceit and deceit—as though they were innocent bystanders hit by a bus.

Usually, the blamers are unwilling to take responsibility for their role in their mangled affair. Emily said she was hurt when she heard her married lover introduce her to his buddy as his "friend." After their breakup, she said the pain from their separation lasted 15 years—long after he cheated on his wife with other women besides her. Fed up and frustrated, she contacted his wife and gave her audiotapes she had made while they were together. The man's wife tried to commit suicide. Now the man blamed Emily as the evildoer.

When we met, she insisted that she was a victim in this situation, just as this man's wife was. She moaned that she knew men who did leave bad marriages for other women, and why couldn't she be one of them? She continued to think of herself as a victim, and she remained alone, lonely, and not dating at the age of 51.

During our sessions, I told her that she had chosen a married man because there was something within her that shunned closeness. All three players—the man, his wife, and she—knew what was going on, even if it was on a level they chose to bury. But each ignored the realities or the consequences. This guy quickly bounced from Emily to other lovers. He was a cheataholic.

There are always options on how to proceed when you get to your Ah-ha Moment:

1. You can become a woe-begotten "poor me" **VICTIM.** (How depressing is that? You're giving the cheater all the power!)

2. You can become an eye-for-an-eye, take-revenge **FIGHTER.** (How exhausting is

that? You're giving the cheater all the
power!)

3. You can become a take-charge **WINNER.**
   (How powerful is that? You're claiming the
   power that rightfully belongs to you. Yay!!)

I told Emily to get off the victim trail. The fact
that she was choosing to use herself as a martyr for
love was totally her choice—and she needed to take
back her power. She had already been the fighter in
this scenario after she sent her beau's wife their
audiotapes. But now, it was time to admit that 15
years without love was too long.

I clarified that she actually had less love than she
believed she had because her lover was unable to
give her what she said she wanted. Of course, now
that she'd been free from him all these years, I
suggested that she couldn't want love very badly,
because she chose to remain alone. Finally, I
trumpeted, "Your major issue is why YOU chose to
stay, not why your lover chose to cheat."

Obviously, I practice tough love. One of my
graduate students asked why I am so hard on people.
She said, "Isn't it your job to nurse them through
their wounds, and take care of them?" I responded
that I never elected to become a nurse. I am an
educator. My job is to elicit growth by leading
people toward enlightenment. Coddling allows
people to continue to rationalize their harmful and

destructive actions. I help people get out of their own way. Often, that involves making some drastic changes in behavior they have traditionally known and accepted—and that's not comfortable.

♛

Gilda-Gram®
If you always do what you've always done,
you'll always go where you've always gone.

My advice program involves challenging past behaviors that did not work, and learning skills to lighten the current pain. But admitting the truth is not easy for most people, and it is not unusual to get some resistance from those looking to protect their hide. The resistance and protection often come in the form of lies and alibis. The excuse that has gotten the most play in recent times is the one that insists that "we're just friends."

Ahhh, the alibi. "Friends" as mere platonic associations seems to be the most common excuse of cheaters. Whenever a partner sniffs that something is askew, the "F" word becomes the verbal absolution of the person caught with pants around his/her ankles. Wouldn't it be better if people simply said, "We're just friendly—er, VERY friendly, or friendlier than most"?

CHAPTER 13

The Saga Of Grieving Husband

Verbal hoodwinking can only camouflage so much. Eventually, the stains on the dirty laundry won't come out in the wash.

Unfortunately, too many spouses hear the "We're just friends" alibi their partner gives them to explain away their sudden closeness with a new "acquaintance." Grieving Husband (GH) was one such brokenhearted spouse. Three weeks before he contacted me, his said his wife of five years confessed to having an affair with her manager. She said she was developing feelings for him, and at some point, she believed she loved him. GH thought their marriage was intact. Now he knew better. Every spouse senses when something in his/her relationship is out of whack.

♛
Gilda-Gram®
Every partner of a cheataholic KNOWS.

For a long time, GH had a feeling that something was not right in his marriage. Although his wife had never been overly affectionate, in recent times especially, she had begun to put him off more than usual. Yet, she continued to speak glowingly of her boss.

Finally, GH asked outright if anything was going on between them. Her response was the usual, "We're just friends." She further explained that her "friend" made her feel special, and since he was also conveniently rich, she graciously accepted the expensive gifts he routinely bought her. After GH probed more and more, she finally confessed.

Turmoil tore their house apart. Finally, his wife decided that she wanted to be with GH, and that she would look for another job to avoid seeing her lover again. But GH could not erase the image of the two of them having sex. He was unable to focus at work or be affectionate at home. That's when he consulted me.

When he described his "hellish" feelings, he said, "I have tried to be a good husband. I built an extension onto our house, I mow the lawn and tend the garden, I take the kids to school, I often do the laundry, and I'm even attending graduate school to gain career advancement and make more money. But my wife has always complained that I never make decisions on my own, and my decisions only reflect her wants, not my own. Finally, she said I don't earn enough money. When I try to express affection, she pushes me away."

GH had been lonely a long time before his wife took up with her manager. Only, he didn't admit that the signs were what they actually were.

As the couple began to discuss what happened to their promise to live "happily ever after," GH's wife told him that her affair with her boss was just a fling. She got hooked on the attention that she felt was lacking at home. Like so many cuckolded mates, GH thought he was doing all the right things to make his wife and family happy. He sadly confessed, "I love my wife, but she really damaged me."

A partner may not know the details of exactly what's going on, but GH admitted to suspecting something was not right in his marriage. After someone admits this, my next question is, "What did you do about your suspicion? Did you ignore your gut feelings, hoping they would go away, or did you confront your wife about what you were feeling at home?" Like too many, GH let his feelings ride until he could no longer ignore the truth.

170

The part of GH's story that was really upsetting to me was how he described himself as "damaged." This raises the question of how much power we are willing to allow someone to wield over us.

♛

Gilda-Gram®
It's too dangerous to give someone power
over how you feel about yourself.

The first thing we needed to work on was GH's feelings about whom he was as a man, independent of how he performed as a husband.

♛

Gilda-Gram®
If you don't respect yourself,
no one else will.

GH needed to pump up his self-confidence and heal the "damage." Then both he and his wife needed to feel they were equal contributors to their union. It was time for GH to get a backbone and to get a life!

♛

Gilda-Gram®
Every healthy relationship
must begin with self-respect.

YOUR CHEATER KEEPS CHEATING
—AND YOU'RE STILL THERE!

I told GH that he should not feel the need to justify himself or his earning capacity to a wife who allegedly loves him.

An affair can either be a wake-up call for lasting marriage, or a goodnight kiss for deadly sleep. Whichever this pair chose would take a lot of effort. Each needed to re-establish new means of expressing his/her passions.

CHAPTER 14

Is Sexless Friendship Possible?

If we were to take the "we're just friends" phrase literally, it would mean platonic buddies would be happy to include their mates in their new "friend"-ships. My friend, Ellen, heard the "we're just friends" phrase from her physicist husband, but he seemed to avoid including Ellen into the "friendly" mix he enjoyed with his playmate. Grieving Husband heard the excuse from his wife cheating with her boss, but he never received an invitation to join Wife and Boss for a "friendly" dinner. Bill Clinton used the phrase to describe his relationship with Monica Lewinsky, and the world knows how that "friendship" nearly brought down a government.

Despite all the denials and disavowals, the "Harry-Met-Sally" school of thought claims that inevitable sexual tension between our plugs and outlets makes platonic friendship impossible. Maybe

173

we should examine the minds of the commitment-averse to understand why.

A study from Johns Hopkins University suggests that temporary amnesia is a potential side effect of top-down sex. (Men's Health Magazine claims the number of manly thrusts required for a 10-minute sex session is a whopping 500!) My published analysis of American Woman Magazine's national sex survey found that females most favored this man-on-top thrusting position. So perhaps that's why men bearing down can't remember what women underneath can. *Like, maybe who's a "friend" and who's a "lover"?*

As we age, the terms "girlfriend" and "boyfriend" seem trifling, and "significant other" is contrived. So, the F-word may be a suitable remedy for relationships just beginning. However, in already-established partnerships, there's often one person galled by the term's use. Like the woman introduced as "my friend" by the guy with whom she'd been living for three years, or the love struck man called "my friend" while meeting the husband of the woman with whom he'd been having an affair.

If we removed the F-word from our vocabularies, this might bust up convenient amnesia, but then, which cover would people have when they want to conceal their indiscretions?

Does our vocabulary have another term to describe our nonsexual connections? Part of the excitement of cheating is the sneaking around. The "friendship" word may actually add to the drama—like when a person openly introduces his/her lover with the lower tier title of "friend" to his/her real friends.

Feeling "betrayed" was Gail's description of her two-year relationship with Lee. Fed up with being relegated to the status of a buddy, she decided to play Lee's own words back for him to hear. As she headed to the airport on a business trip, the driver of a limo company she had used for years picked her up. She and the driver had established good rapport over the course of Gail's patronage.

When Lee walked her to the car, she introduced the driver as a "friend" to her "friend" Lee. For the first time, Lee heard that he and the driver were on the same casual footing. Lee stammered, "I'm not Gail's friend. I'm her b-b-b-boyfriend," a term he had adamantly protested, saying it was too juvenile for an adult male. Suddenly, Lee was confronted with his own medicine—and he discovered that he didn't like its taste.

Sure, if we removed the F-word we might have to become honest. Truth in advertising? While this might be a refreshing relationship concept, honesty would reduce the high generated by all the sneaking around. For many, if the excitement suddenly dulled, how much benefit would the cheating offer?

American Demographics/Synovate found that 18-to-24-year-olds were four times as likely as people over 55 to have a best friend of the opposite sex, and adults 25 to 34, have a one in 10 chance of making someone from the opposite sex a friend. So, the younger demographics find it easier to maintain friendships devoid of sex. But despite these findings, there's a great deal of tension regarding this topic.

Dear Dr. Gilda,

I am a 30-year-old guy. I just read your response to one of your women followers about leaving her husband because she's "fallen in love" with one of her so-called male friends. First, this is why men HATE letting their women have male "friends." It's NEVER just friends. Either one or both have secret motives in mind. As with this slut, she leaves her husband one day, and the next day she's screwing her so-called "friend." Second, men who have women for friends look at them as easy prey. I know of many guys who love this situation just to get free rides off another man's woman.

This is exactly why my wife knows better than to even try to contact another man, let alone try to become friends with one!!!! If women didn't have

*what they do between their legs, they would be of no
use to men as "friends."*

Keeping My Wife on a Tight Leash

Ouch! I have no idea how long this dude's
marriage has lasted, but with that attitude, anytime
soon, his wife may just break her leash and run.
Then he'll probably blame everyone else, including
me, for her newfound freedom and independence. He
will never believe it had anything to do with his
incarceration of an adult human being.

A study of 137 couples out of the University of
Groningen, Netherlands, found that when couples
became friends before lovers, their relationships
were based on similar personalities, and that factor
creates long-term harmony. Professor of
Communication, Heidi Reeder, points out that there
are three types of attraction that exist between males
and females: sexual, romantic and friendship.
People may feel one or two of these attractions and
not the third. For example, someone may adore his
friend's personality, but not be sexually attracted to
her. Yet, friendship is vital before a love
relationship.

♛
Gilda-Gram®
Friends first, lovers later.

Someone once called love as "friendship on fire."
If all three of Reeder's attractions are not in place,

there is little hope for a lasting relationship. After the heat of the moment has been doused by cold-water reality, and Passion Deprivation sets in, it is the friendship that carries the future.

Friendships with the opposite sex serve some distinct positive purposes. Men want female friends they can talk to, and since they tend to avoid emotional closeness with other men, a woman they can trust would be a good person to whom to reveal their emotions. Women want male friends they can share their intimate emotions with, who will serve as sounding boards for their relationships with other men. It's almost like trying out some parts of their emotional repertoire before they enact them in the real world.

So, there is a possibility for friendship with a member of the opposite sex. But which one? Can it be an ex you once casually dated? Could it be someone with whom you were in love?

If all three of Reeder's elements are not in place in BOTH parties, there is a good chance that platonic friendship could exist. But both people must know what they feel and be willing to honestly share those feelings, regardless of the hurt they might inflict. Overall, can two exes ever be "just friends"? The answer is a resounding "no" if time has not passed. Becoming friends at the wrong time for the wrong reasons will undoubtedly end up hurting at least one of a pair.

Some exes feign an interest in a friendship in hopes of getting back together. Or some want friendship with their ex to avoid the bad breakup feelings from lingering. If enough time has not gone by, a person might be hurt when his/her ex couples with someone new, and even discusses it with him/her. One never knows how his/her ex-lover would perform as a future platonic friend.

Getting over an ex you had deep emotional ties to isn't quick or easy. Unfortunately, there's no getting around the necessary passing of time.

♛

Gilda-Gram®
The opposite of love is not hate;
it's apathy.

Only after you have dispelled your loving (and hateful) emotions can you feel apathetic about a love affair with an ex. That's the only time you can freely create an entirely new format that exists for friendship that will exclude the vestiges of the past.

When you have a clean slate, if you want to be friends with an ex, sit face-to-face for an honest "exchange." Choose to be *friendly towards* rather than *friends with* each other. Or you may decide simply to be on good terms when you run into each other, with nothing more.

You can select from any number of alternatives that rule out breaking your heart for a second time. If you're already involved with someone new, how will that person feel about your now-platonic friendship? Will your mate believe you're "just friends," or will s/he think you're cheating?

CHAPTER 15

"Friends" Vs. "Friends With Benefits"

I learned the phrase "friends with benefits" when I was the Love Doc for MTV Online. "Friends with benefits" is a practice that describes someone who is willing to "put out" to "fit in." It started when teen girls offered oral sex with no strings, and no commitment. While on face value, they came across as nonchalant and in control, in truth, they wanted the recipient of their offerings to care for them. As soon as they found that their efforts did not win them the love they wanted, they were distraught. It breaks my heart to read their emails of regret, anger, and being had.

Now the "friends with benefits" practice has expanded into the adult sector. People may agree to partner with someone, but they say upfront that it must be without commitment. Or sometimes, they sleep with a partner, and they say nothing about the future. At first, a partner may accept an affair at face value, but over time, there may be an unwillingness to continue the status quo. If someone's bedmate still wants to remain "friends with benefits," the other party may be emotionally wounded.

Gina was going through a painful second divorce, mostly because her husband's libido couldn't keep up with hers. He criticized that she was too demanding, and she retaliated with accusations that he was asexual. Finally, in the last two years of their marriage, they'd only been intimate once.

After many confrontations, Gina's husband admitted it was because she'd had breast cancer and was going through the process of breast reconstruction that he didn't find her attractive anymore. She was stunned by his shallowness, and she wondered if other guys would view her the same way. Her self-esteem was shattered.

She quickly became involved with a few men, none of whom were bothered by her scars or implants. Her self-esteem began to return, and that's when she met Robert, who had had a vasectomy, so she felt there was no need to use a condom. Their sexual compatibility was explosive.

Gina boldly said she was just looking for a "friend with benefits." But she quickly discovered that Robert only wanted benefits, with no friendship.

She silently hoped that time and patience would bring him around. *Many women do that, as they wait, unfulfilled!* By sheer accident, she discovered that he was seeing two other women at the same time while he was seeing her. Ten weeks later, she contracted herpes.

Statistically, one in four women and one in five men have genital herpes. Ninety percent of them don't know it. Gina was devastated. First the breast cancer, then the ex-husband's humiliating dismissal of her attractiveness, and now this! Robert insisted the disease didn't come from him. Then he stopped taking Gina's calls.

Frankly, I have never seen the concept of "friends with benefits" work; one person usually wants deeper friendship while the other wants greater benefits. The only kind of relationship that works is one in which both parties share the same goal. Quickie sex used to pump up shattered self-esteem can backfire. And one of the backfires is a sexually transmitted disease.

While divorcing Liza Minelli, David Gest claimed that she had herpes, but didn't reveal it until after they married. He claimed their prenup should be declared null and void based on fraud, even though he claimed to be herpes-free. While the lawyers battled out this ugly $10 million divorce, Liza's private health information was embarrassingly dragged through the media as the sparring partners sued each other.

Atlanta Falcons quarterback Michael Vick settled out of court with a partner who alleged she contracted herpes from him, and that he knew of his condition beforehand. But in 1995, former NBA star, Dennis Rodman, fared better when an Atlanta jury found him not guilty of knowingly passing herpes to a former cheerleader. In 1996, a New York woman won $600,000 from her millionaire ex-husband, who reportedly slept with prostitutes, knowingly gave her herpes, and failed to disclose either fact.

An estimated 80% of Americans carry the virus HSV-1, which manifests as oral cold sores. And 20% carry HSV-2, a 30% increase since the 1970s, according to the Centers for Disease Control. Anyone who knows s/he carries the disease has a moral and legal obligation to share that information, unless s/he wants to risk being sued.

Many people with herpes, AIDS, and other STDs never transmit them to their intimate partners because they are careful. If there is a silver lining to any of this, some of these diseases may actually keep people from jumping into the sack indiscriminately. Why play under the guise of "friends with benefits" anyway, and attract unworthy partners who will only let you down?

It used to be only women who longed for closeness, but these days, my inbox is filled with email from men who are just as hurt when affection doesn't follow the sex. Things can get mighty messy when a hurt love, whether male or female, is rebuked. Consider the movie, "Fatal Attraction," where the cheating husband enjoyed a weekend romp with a single woman. When he was ready to dismiss her after his wife and child returned from the country, the single woman went crazy, physically turning on the man and his family in a bloody, near-fatal attack.

In discussing that movie with many men, I found that their level of fear had really been raised as a result of that flick.

Janice and James, both in their 40s, were great friends over the course of five years. They hung out together, they went to each other's family gatherings, and they cried on each other's shoulder when one of their love affairs went sour. They just adored each other's company, and there was never the thought of them taking their connection into any other arena. I met this couple at a party. Believe it or not, they had just become newlyweds.

I asked, "What made you change from platonic friendship to lovers?" Janice laughed and said, "We really and truly weren't aware of what was happening. Actually, it was our friends who noticed that our feelings were deeper than we even thought. Our friends pushed us to at least consider more. As soon as we did, we said, 'Wow!'"

This was the most jubilant couple I had seen in a long time. As my Gilda-Gram® prescribes, love is best when friendship precedes it. But it's stories such as Janice's and James' that send even the most trusting lover or spouse into skeptical disarray, to hear that a partner's innocent friendship blossomed into a cheating liaison.

The Internet has made it easy to find a lost love of years past, and school reunions can accelerate the pace. They all initially renew friendships. But lost-and-found emails and meetings can be hazardous to people who are supposedly happily married. Past relationships hold the memory of youthful dreams and glory days that aging folks may want to recapture.

There is also the "autobiographical memory bump," the clarity of memories forged during times of early love, which reflect a simpler life with fewer issues. And finally, there is what anthropologist, Helen Fisher, calls "frustration attraction," a rendition of "absence makes the heart grow fonder." Fisher hypothesizes that dopamine-producing neurons, which stimulate the motivation to pursue a lover, actually increase when that lover is gone.

Nancy Kalish, an expert on rekindled romance, has found that lost-and-found romances are surprisingly successful if both people are free. In a sample of 1,000 lovers, ages 18 to 95, 75% remained together after a decade. And their divorce rate was only 1.5% after four years of marriage. But Kalish cautions that in her latest sample, over 60% of lost-love reunions involve affairs—and sometimes they don't end so happily.

You see, as much as people use the "just friends" cover, yes, friendship can turn to love—and actually, that's when it's best. That's one reason that Kalish's findings in lost-love romances show marital success. In contrast, when a relationship begins with sex first, when that passion naturally wilts, what foundation does a couple have to fall back on to re-build what they had?

That was precisely the situation that Sally found herself in when her married and divorcing boyfriend cheated on her. She had been with him for nine months, knowing he was married. But she rationalized, "I don't fool myself that this started out as anything but sex and an 'exit affair' for him."

The sex must have been mind-blowing, because he ended up leaving his wife two months into their union. However, as he filed for divorce, and began living with Sally, he was growing more and more depressed. He was feeling guilt-ridden over their

187

affair, and terrified about the prospect of leaving behind the only life he'd known for 10 years.

Her lover-turned-live-in went on anti-depressants, and their sex life stopped due to the side effects of the drugs. He also stopped talking to her about important things they used to share.

To deaden his pain, he began trolling the Internet for other lovers. As soon as Sally discovered this, she kicked him out and ended things with him. That terrified him even more. He told her he wanted to salvage their relationship, acknowledging his pattern of avoidance and running off to other women. He claimed he wanted to change.

Sally told me, "I don't understand the reasoning behind his feeling depressed and starting another affair." I did. I explained that her boyfriend was a cheataholic. While he wasn't aware of it, he continued to seek a new sex partner each time he felt agitated or worthless.

Sally didn't know what to do. She said, "Part of me wants to work things through with him, but I'm terrified he will cheat again—maybe next time after we're married or have kids—and that would devastate me all over again. Another part of me feels weak for not writing him off altogether, because I don't want to be a doormat."

The woman wanted to know whether there was something wrong with her for wanting to save their relationship. She also wanted to know if someone with a history of cheating (before her, with her, and on her) was even capable of (or likely to) change. EVERYONE ASKS THAT!!

Finally, she asked that if she went back to him, wouldn't she be just giving him permission to do it all again? She said she was desperate to get her head "back on straight."

I have observed that every derailed relationship is fixable IF both parties want to fix it and IF they are willing to do the arduous work required after such a deep wound. I told Sally that she can work on cheat-proofing this partnership or any other she intends to have in the future—if she follows my advice.

♕
Gilda-Gram®
Everyone who touches us teaches us.
Apply each lesson as you learn it.

CONCLUSION

I'm in the therapy business, so, of course, I believe that EVERYTHING is fixable IF two partners are willing and able. I believe that betrayal issues can be beneficial to relationships on the fence because they push the envelope.

After a shocking betrayal is when you are pressed to take stock of what you have, and work on it, or decide to call it quits. I have seen relationships become stronger as a result of working through their betrayal issues. And I have also seen couples fall apart.

NO MATTER WHAT COURSE A COUPLE CHOOSES, LASY LOVE CANNOT CONTINUE—AND THAT'S A GOOD THING!

The ultimate decision depends on the two people, it depends on whether they are willing to turn their obstacle into an opportunity, and it depends on whether they deeply want to sustain their relationship *above all else*—including their anger, their hostility, and their "gotcha" mentality.

It is not necessary to forget—because you actually do want to remember the circumstances that led to your relationship's derailment, so it won't repeat itself. But it is absolutely mandatory that you forgive—whether you choose to continue the partnership or not. Forgiving is not for your mate; it's for YOU!

♛

Gilda-Gram®
Forgive, but don't forget
what got you into your jam.

Once you forgive, you can glide into whatever status you choose to pursue, with whomever you select. Forgiveness paves the way for your next couple status. This time, it will be founded on strength, not on disabling hurt that will prevent you from living happily, perhaps not ever after, but at least for now . . .

♦♦♦

For additional questions, contact me at **www.DrGilda.com**

Love (of course),
Dr. Gilda

YOUR CHEATER KEEPS CHEATING
—AND YOU'RE STILL THERE!

♦♦♦

Benefit from Dr. Gilda's personal Advice &
Coaching

www.DrGilda.com

♦♦♦

MORE BOOKS BY DR. GILDA

Dr. Gilda's Self-Worth Series

-- "I'm Worth Loving! Here's Why."
-- "Ask for What You Want—AND GET IT!
-- "How to Be a Worry-Free Woman"

Dr. Gilda's Relationship Series

--8 Steps to a Sizzling Marriage
--8 Tips to Understand the Opposite Sex
--10 Questions Single Women Should Never
Ask & 10 They Should
--10 Signs of a Cheater-to-Be

Dr. Gilda's Fidelity Series

--Why Your Cheater Keeps Cheating—and
You're Still There
--How to WIN When Your Mate Cheats—2nd
Edition

--99 Prescriptions for Fidelity: Your Rx for Trust

Dr. Gilda's Business Book

--One Up Strategies Business Schools Don't Teach

ALSO

--Don't Bet on the Prince! How to Have the Man You Want by Betting on Yourself

--Don't Lie on Your Back for a Guy Who Doesn't Have Yours

♦♦♦

DR. GILDA CARLE (Ph.D.) is the media's Go-To Relationship Expert & Corporate Performance Coach, serving clients worldwide at www.DrGilda.com. As a media personality, she was the therapist on TV's Sally Jessy Raphael show as well as most other TV & news shows, from Howard Stern to Dateline.

She also conducts Relationship Wellness training at medical facilities, including Columbia University Medical Center. As President of non-profit Country Cures® at www.CountryCures.org, she uniquely applies Country Music to empower Homeless Female Veterans.

She is a product spokesperson (Hallmark, Harlequin, Sprint, Cottonelle, Galderma Pharmaceuticals, Match.com), keynote speaker,

YOUR CHEATER KEEPS CHEATING
—AND YOU'RE STILL THERE!

Professor Emerita of Business, and author of 17 books, including "Don't Bet on the Prince!" (test question on "Jeopardy"), "How to WIN When Your Mate Cheats" (literary award winner from London Book Festival), and "Don't Lie on Your Back for a Guy Who Doesn't Have Yours" (featured on National Enquirer's Health Page).

Dr. Gilda wrote the weekly "30-Second Therapist" column for the Today Show, the "Ask Dr. Gilda" column for Match.com, and she was the therapist in HBO's Emmy Award winner, "Telling Nicholas," featured on Oprah. She hosted Fox's "Dr. Gilda" TV show pilot, MTV's "Love Doc," and TV shows on Trinity Broadcasting Network.

———————————

Reach Dr. Gilda at

www.DrGilda.com

or

www.CountryCures.org